Embracing Challenges resets our view of conflict as a constructive dialectic process founded on sound teaching principles and flexible methods. Oken-Wright's transcribed conversations perfectly exemplify her message, and the chapter summaries invite the reader to think critically.

George E. Forman, Ph.D., *Emeritus Professor, University of Massachusetts, Amherst*

In this book, Pam is our pedagogical companion. She encourages and supports our learning about what it means to stand alongside children and, together, explore the foundational question, "How does life work?" Pam offers generous and clear guidance about how to cultivate the cognitive and emotional flexibility that allows teachers and children to embrace "good conflict," sticking with each other and with their shared undertakings even when—especially when!—they encounter uncertainty, divergent perspectives, and disequilibrium. This book is a necessary text for our times.

Ann Pelo, *Co-author of* From Teaching to Thinking: A Pedagogy for Reimagining Our Work

Pam invites us to explore some of the most feared and avoided terrain in the education landscape, acting as a trusted companion on what turns out to be an exciting and meaningful journey. She provides a wide variety of practical tools, and shares stories that inspire us to appreciate the beauty in the complexity and uncertainty of working with young children. This book encourages us to do the difficult and brave work of embracing conflict, allowing us to strengthen the agency we need to become the teachers we aspire to be.

Susan Harris MacKay, *The Center and Studio for Playful Inquiry*

Embracing Challenges in Early Childhood Education

Embracing Challenges in Early Childhood Education is a key resource for early childhood educators, especially those inspired by the Reggio Emilia approach or other inquiry-based, social-constructivist models. It answers the important question teachers face when they come up against challenges in their work with children: "What do I do now?" Not a how-to guide for implementing the Reggio Emilia philosophy, nor simply an inspirational read, this book encourages reflection, innovation, and responsive teaching while offering practical insights, thoughtful frameworks, and real-world guidance to help educators navigate inevitable challenges in ways that honor their creativity and intelligence along with that of the children in their care. This book is essential reading for early childhood educators, pedagogical consultants, and school leaders and is also a valuable theoretical resource for Reggio-inspired study groups committed to enhancing their educational practices.

Pam Oken-Wright, M.Ed., is a pedagogical consultant and author who worked with young children as a teacher-researcher for 37 years.

Other Eye on Education Books
Available from Routledge
(www.routledge.com/eyeoneducation)

Reimagining the Role of Teachers in Nature-based Learning: Helping Children be Curious, Confident, and Caring
Rachel Larimore and Claire Warden

Promoting Language and Early Literacy Development: Practical Insights from a Parent Researcher
Pamela Beach

Teaching Higher-Order Thinking to Young Learners, K–3: How to Develop Sharp Minds for the Disinformation Age
Steffen Saifer

Everyday STEAM for the Early Childhood Classroom: Integrating the Arts into STEM Teaching
Margaret Loring Merrill

A New Vision for Early Childhood: Rethinking Our Relationships with Young Children
Noah Hichenberg

Embracing Challenges in Early Childhood Education

Flexible Protocols for the Thinking Teacher

Pam Oken-Wright

Routledge
Taylor & Francis Group
NEW YORK AND LONDON

Designed cover image: Katharina Geissbuehler

First published 2025
by Routledge
605 Third Avenue, New York, NY 10158

and by Routledge
4 Park Square, Milton Park, Abingdon, Oxon, OX14 4RN

Routledge is an imprint of the Taylor & Francis Group, an informa business

© 2025 Taylor & Francis

The right of Pam Oken-Wright to be identified as author of this work has been asserted in accordance with sections 77 and 78 of the Copyright, Designs and Patents Act 1988.

All rights reserved. No part of this book may be reprinted or reproduced or utilized in any form or by any electronic, mechanical, or other means, now known or hereafter invented, including photocopying and recording, or in any information storage or retrieval system, without permission in writing from the publishers.

Trademark notice: Product or corporate names may be trademarks or registered trademarks, and are used only for identification and explanation without intent to infringe.

ISBN: 9781041038290 (hbk)
ISBN: 9781041038276 (pbk)
ISBN: 9781003625568 (ebk)

DOI: 10.4324/9781003625568

Typeset in Palatino
by KnowledgeWorks Global Ltd.

To the hundreds of children who were my joy and my teachers over the years, some of whom populate the stories in this book.

Contents

Meet the Author xii
Acknowledgments xiii

Introduction 1
How to Use This Book 8

I: The Child, the Teacher, and Conflict as Gift and Challenge 11

1 **The Beauty of Conflict** 13

2 **Who Is the Child?** 18
   What Do We Hope for Children and the World They Live In? 19

3 **Who Is the Teacher?** 27
   The Thinking Teacher 28
   Research with Children 30
   Consider This 32

4 **The Role of Inner and External Conflict in Teaching and Learning** 33
   Inner Conflict for the Learner 33
   Inner and External Conflict for Teachers 35
   The Inner Conflict of Uncertainty 39
   Shame in "Failure" 40
   Conflict Around Values, Practice, and Expectations 40
   Disagreements with Colleagues 42
   Consider This 44

5 **Challenges to Pedagogical Flow** 45
   Points of Conflict 47

  Teacher Scripts..48
  Flexible Protocols as an Alternative to Scripts 51
  Consider This 54

II: Flexible Protocols: Tools for the Back Pocket of the Thinking Teacher 55

6 The Environment and Small Systems 57
  A Rich Environment 58
  Developing a Culture of Community..................................60
  Constructing Agreements 65
  Collaborative Management 68
  "They Won't Let Me Play" 69
  The Planning Protocol..71
  Schedules for Deep Engagement 73
  Work in Progress 74
  Consider This 75

7 Flow Challenge: Social Conflict. 77
  The Adult-Child Interaction Continuum 79
  Using the Protocol..81
  Consider This 89

8 Conversations for the Co-Construction of Theory. 90
  The Power of Conversation 90
  Co-Constructing Theory 91
  Stages of Participation in Group Conversations..................98
  The Teacher as Curious Listener 105
  Facilitating Conversation...107
  "Incorrect" Theories 111
  Developing a Culture of Conversation.............................113
  The Conversation Protocol 114
  Consider This 118

9 Flow Challenge: Cognitive Conflict in Play and Conversation 119
  Conflict in Conversation 124
  It's a Crowd!..125

  Difficult Topics in Conversation 125
  Cognitive Conflict 131
  Consider This 132

10 Flow Challenge: The Project Stalls 133
  The Investigation Protocol 133

11 The Cardinal Story 157
  Do We Want to Catch the Cardinals? 157
  The Children Take the Perspective of the Birds 158
  Proposing to Hide Behind a Tree 158
  To Disguise as a Cardinal ... or Not 158
  Luring Cardinals with Images of Other Cardinals 159
  Consider This 171

12 Points of Conflict in Children's Research 172
  Layers of Attraction 174
  Consider This 182

13 Flow Challenge: Points of Conflict in
  Representation 183
  The Shared Idea Protocol 186
  The Shared Drawing Protocol 188
  The Study Protocol 190

14 The Clay Horse 199
  Consider This 207

  Conclusion 208
  Resources 210
  For Those Who Are New to the Reggio Emilia Philosophy 210
  Resources for Inspiration about Learning Spaces 210

Meet the Author

Pam Oken-Wright, M.Ed., is a pedagogical consultant and author who worked with young children as a teacher-researcher for 37 years. She has studied the Reggio Emilia philosophy since 1990 and enjoys supporting educators on their journeys exploring this most joyful (and complex!) way of teaching and learning. Pam has traveled internationally to consult and give workshops and keynotes. She is the author of *"Mommy, They're Taking Away My Imagination:" Educating Your Young Child at Home* and has authored many chapters and articles. She publishes a blog at pokenwright.com.

Pam, lives with her husband and three dogs in Richmond, Virginia.

Acknowledgments

Many thanks:

To Susan Harris MacKay and Matt Karlsen, who reminded me that I had a body of work I needed to share.

To Ann Pelo and Dorothy Suskind, whose thoughtful reading and feedback made this a much better book.

To Jen Miller, who contributed to this book her insight into what it's like to make courageous changes in perspective and practice in her teaching.

To my assistants/co-teachers over the years who helped test out the protocols in this book and to whom credit for some of the photos is owed: Marsha Alexander, Rita Ashlock, Susan Croft, Katie Erb, Katharina Geissbuehler, Ashley Holden, Kit Leppert, Jan Locher, Frances Martin, Susan Verghis, and Tamra Wilt.

And

With eternal gratitude to the educators of Reggio Emilia, who have led the way for the thinking teacher.

Introduction

It's St. Patrick's Day. The children have come to junior kindergarten with stories about green water in their toilets at home, sequins all over the floor, and other magic that they find intriguing, especially since they never saw the agent of the mischief. Once at school, 3 five-year-old girls set out to construct a trap to catch the leprechaun their parents told them was responsible for the mischief. They wanted to build one trap together, but there were three minds involved, each with a different idea for the trap. From experience, they knew that drawing a plan could help them understand and be understood. So, they got a piece of paper and started a collaborative drawing of the trap. They soon encountered a point of conflict. As they were wont to do, they stopped to talk about it.

Abby: We have to make it really secure so they (the leprechaun) will die.
Honor: OK, the knife(pointing to a figure on the drawing).
Maggie: No, we're not gonna cut their heads off!
Abby: Yes, that's a really good idea.

Another child at the table commented in a silly tone of voice, which distracted the trap-makers from their intent momentarily.

Teacher: So, what's the plan for the trap so far?
Honor: There's a knife…
Maggie: No, we're not going to cut their heads off!

Abby brings two more pieces of paper to the table.

Honor: No, that's not how you collaborate, with different pieces of paper.

(Pause) I have an idea, I have an idea. How about we all draw pictures, and then we can vote?

Abby: OK, I'm already drawing.

Maggie: I like your picture, Honor. I vote for that one. Get the key (to open the trap) on there.

Honor: And the knife that hurts them (spoken with a sly smile)?

Maggie: And not kill them.

The cognitive conflict about whether the trap the girls planned should kill the leprechaun or just trap him served a number of purposes for their project. It solidified their collaboration and let them clarify a shared image of the trap. And the compromise allowed them to resume their design work, all without cost to their relationship. How is it that five-year-olds are able to lean into conflict, find pleasure in collaboration, and balance a relationship that is important to them with multiple perspectives? That is what this book is about.

These days, when so much of the public discourse revolves around disagreement, dichotomies, "sides," and othering (powell & Menendian, 2024), we are sorely missing the disposition to see all the complexities and perspectives of the other as opportunities to learn or accomplish something. Our tendency to simplify each other has been supported by those who can benefit from dividing us. It doesn't make us happy, does it? How did we get here? And what can be done about it?

Maggie, Honor, and Abby work through a moment of cognitive conflict.

As an early childhood educator pondering these questions, I admit to some bias. I can't help but wonder: what if belonging were a fundamental principle in our pedagogy? What if we adults learned to value conflict for how it can support learning and create community, and what if we shifted our values and practices so that the children we teach learn to think (and not just regurgitate facts)? Would they be as easily swayed by emotion as some of their elders seem to be? Is there an antidote to the extreme othering we are experiencing now? What if children left school really knowing how it feels to belong and didn't need to exclude others to feel it? What if teachers and children could walk confidently into good conflict knowing that it would be a safe and pleasurable endeavor?

The children in the leprechaun trap vignette came to our all-girls independent school in September, still four years old, without the skills and dispositions they used while planning the trap. Before they came to junior kindergarten, they had become accustomed to having a teacher or parent solve their problems for them, and any time they found themselves in cognitive or social conflict at the beginning of the year, tempers flared, and tears were common. But during our year together, the children experienced the power of conversation and negotiation. They found pleasure in collaboration. They learned to use drawing for planning, clarity, and expression and for support in the face of cognitive conflict during their collaboration with others. They might disagree, but they could enjoy the banter because they didn't find conflict threatening. They were not afraid of losing or harming relationships or their identities because of disagreements. They…and their teachers…had learned to use challenges (like the many forms of conflict that arise in a community of learners) for good.

The educators in Reggio Emilia speak of the value of "confronto" in education, referring to cognitive conflict, generative discourse, or co-constructing knowledge and theory by working together through challenges. Part I of this book is about confronto, which we might consider "good conflict," full of challenges that help us grow, inform our worldview, and engender change. It is about internal cognitive conflict for teachers and children and why it is a necessary condition for learning. It is about the opportunity such challenges represent and what teachers can do to embrace it. It is about social conflict among children, among teachers, and between children and teachers and how one might come through it richer and with relationships intact. It is about embracing the uncertainty (inner conflict) that inevitably arises when a classroom is a place of children's research.

In Chapter 2, I once again borrow from our esteemed colleagues in Reggio Emilia and ask, "Who is the child?" We want to be clear about what we believe about children and what we want for them. It is the foundation of all we do in education. An image of the child as strong and capable must be accompanied by a changed image of the teacher (Chapter 3). Is she a cog who follows the instructions of the school machine or a thinking teacher who gets to use her intelligence, creativity, and initiative in the classroom and uses conflict for good? Almost all the teachers I know are smart, creative, caring, and insightful individuals who are far more capable than they are led to believe; they don't always get to express those attributes in their teaching. This book provides a way forward to a classroom where children and teachers can express (and use) their intelligence in a way traditional schooling has made seem unattainable. It is not. Chapter 2 also proposes a set of dispositions and habits of mind for children and teachers toward that end and a statement of what we might hope for children and the world they live in.

Chapter 4 is about how conflict affects and supports learners and teachers. Teachers in Reggio-inspired classrooms, identified as teacher-researchers, have a different role from that of their more traditional colleagues. Particular work encounters particular challenges that require more than easy fixes adopted from a teacher's manual or how-to blog. Teachers who have recently begun participating in children's research may find that the scripts they found helpful before no longer fit the bill. They may even be inconsistent with the teacher's values and image of the child. Some may find themselves at an in-between place, not satisfied with old strategies but still needing some support in their transition. This book offers that support.

Chapter 5 introduces pedagogical "Flow." Flow is a state in which we become so deeply engaged in what we are doing that time slips away. Children play in a state of flow. Your days with children in the classroom can be spent in a similar state of flow, but only if it is not interrupted by moments of emotional conflict. When cognitive or social conflict arises but those involved have strategies for using it constructively, flow in play and research can be maintained or, if temporarily interrupted, restored. Chapter 4 also describes "teacher scripts," limited mechanisms that tell teachers what to do in response to challenges in the classroom in a defined way. Teachers working within a more traditional paradigm tend to collect such scripts, which may give them a sense of certainty and security against the unknown. An educator likely will chafe against many such scripts once he has adjusted his image of the child, of teaching, and of himself as a teacher. He will not run from the unknown (an internal point of conflict); rather, he embraces it with the expectation that something wonderful will happen along the way. He also wants to approach pedagogical challenges in a way that preserves the child's sense of agency and belonging. Old scripts don't address these points of conflict in a way that maintains those important ways of being, nor do they take advantage of the ways in which conflict supports learning. But what will the thinking teacher use as support if he eschews old scripts? If his work is too big for old scripts to work? If they don't align with his values anymore?

It would be wonderful if every teacher had a pedagogical consultant/companion with her at every moment to offer collaboration as problems arise and not get in the way when they don't. But that is unrealistic. Where a teacher needs support or reassurance but doesn't have human support, or when colleagues need a scaffold they can build upon, flexible protocols, introduced in Chapter 5, provide guidance without being prescriptive. Flexible protocols are open-ended systems that a teacher can use to address pedagogical sticking points, either as they arise or to head them off. Rather than give a short answer to an internal or external point of conflict, flexible protocols offer a long-form map that can broaden the canvas of learning. That is, in using flexible protocols, the educator uses challenges as an asset to the teaching and learning processes. The conflict becomes the curriculum; working through it enriches and educates all involved.

The protocols in this book came from my practice over decades as responses to challenges I experienced in my own teaching. The more my practice reflected a strong image of the children I worked with, the greater my understanding of my role as a facilitator of the learning children were already doing when I met them. I no longer saw myself as a director, controller, or font of all knowledge. I found myself dissatisfied with the old assumptions and scripts I encountered at the beginning of my career. They were just too limiting. So, the protocols evolved over time as we worked our way through sticking points, always keeping in mind the seminal questions, "What do we want for the children, not just today, but for their whole lives?" and "How can we create the world they deserve?"

Where scripts are inflexible mechanisms, flexible protocols are frameworks that are bendable to your setting, to you, and to the children you teach. Though the protocols in this book are for teachers, many are also protocols for children, in that as the teacher uses a protocol to support children's negotiation with ideas, materials, and other people, children embrace the strategies. In time, as their competence and confidence grow, they begin to use the protocols for their own purposes.

Each chapter in Part II addresses a different challenge to pedagogical Flow, with a corresponding protocol. Chapter 6 describes the environment's role in children's research and introduces some of the small systems I used in my classroom. Small Systems are narrower in scope than the other protocols in this book but no less powerful. Examples are constructing agreements, a system for "they won't let me play," schedules for deep engagement, and planning with children.

The flow challenge in Chapter 7 is social conflict. The premise of this chapter is that with support, children can find and use their voices to make their needs, desires, and feelings known to each other, and they can learn to respond to the language and feelings of the other. In this way, social conflict can be resolved without shame or a sense of helplessness. The protocol to support all this is the Adult Child Interaction Continuum

(ACIC), which turns children toward each other in times of conflict and supports repairing damaged relationships. When using the ACIC, teachers can learn where and how children need support to negotiate through social conflict. With the protocol, teachers can offer children enough support to articulate their opinions and emotions and respond to the expression of other children without giving too much support or becoming emotionally involved themselves. The ACIC helps keep social conflict cognitive so that everyone involved can think and learn from the conflict experience.

The thinking teacher knows that having good conversations with children is a vital element in their research. He also knows how challenging that can be at times. Chapter 8 describes conversations for the co-construction of theory and how you might include them in your pedagogy. The chapter addresses stages of participation in group conversations and what a teacher can do to enable and support sustained dialogue. Here we meet the Conversation Protocol, which offers practical advice about having good conversations for the co-construction of theory.

Chapter 9 addresses cognitive conflict as it occurs in play and conversation. Cognitive conflict typically does not involve someone taking someone else's toy or turn; rather, it usually arises when children disagree about ideas, research, and plans. It happens when children's theories collide during a class conversation or children working on a collaborative representation disagree about how to proceed, for example. In conversations for the co-construction of theory, conflict is inevitable and sustaining. Through dialogue, children experience ideas different from their own, and the boundaries of their understanding may stretch. In the same conversation, teachers might be challenged by uncertainty and insecurity ("Where is this conversation going?" "What is my role here?" "What should I do about misconceptions or magical thinking?" and so forth). Chapter 9 addresses these challenges as well as the discomfort and value of tackling difficult topics that arise in class conversations. A teacher may experience trepidation about where the conversation could go or about a reaction from administrators or parents. This is another situation for which there is no viable script. The answer comes through a shift in perspective and a disposition to take a risk that has a high likelihood of yielding something wonderful.

Chapters 10 and 11 address points of conflict in research with children and introduce the Investigation Protocol. This protocol gives educators a framework for collaborating with children in their research. Children's research is wonderfully unpredictable. As such, it is susceptible to all kinds of sticking points that can disrupt pedagogical Flow. For example, investigations may stall or never start; children may get stuck while trying to express their ideas; children and teachers may not know how to proceed with research; disagreements may emerge, and so on. The thinking teacher does not want to resort to old scripts when these things happen. But at times, she may need guidance that preserves her right to deep engagement with the children, to creative problem-solving, and to autonomy in her classroom. From identifying compelling ideas in children's play, conversation, and representation to the role of pedagogical documentation in children's and teachers' learning, the protocol offers insights and practical strategies for accomplishing small and large research projects with children. Chapter 12 offers food for thought about some frequently posed points of conflict teachers have when engaging with children in their research.

Chapters 13 and 14 are about sticking points children (and, therefore, teachers) encounter when representing their thinking with materials. Here, you will find the Shared Idea Protocol, the Shared Drawing Protocol, and the Study Protocol. Like other chapters in the book, these chapters include learning stories from my classroom in which the protocols played a part.

How to Use This Book

I hope that you will use this book however it is useful to you. Some will read it from cover to cover, which, of course, I would love for you to do. But it can be equally useful as a resource for areas in which you have experienced inner or external conflict. You can skip around to find what you need. Feel free to share the protocols with colleagues who have identified common points of conflict in their teaching. Post a protocol to help everyone who works with the children stay on the same page if that's useful. Take the book to your study group and read together a chapter a month. Choose one protocol or small system to take up at a time or plug a protocol into your already successful inquiry-based program. I'd love to know how you have chosen to use the book!

Inspiration for writing this book came from my colleagues Susan Harris MacKay and Matt Karlsen, founders of the Studio for Playful Inquiry. They asked me to have a conversation with them for the participants in the studio. They chose "conflict" as the topic, and I was a bit bewildered. Only once had I published an article about conflict in the classroom…I thought. But, in preparation for the conversation, Susan and Matt mined my writing over decades and found a thread I hadn't named. When I looked back, I realized they were right. So much of my work had to do with harnessing conflict for good. At that point, my plan to write about the flexible protocols I'd created or adapted over the years hooked up with my thinking about conflict, and you have the result in your hands.

Reference

powell, j. a.. & Menendian, S. (2024). *Belonging Without Othering: How We Save Ourselves and the World.* Stanford University Press.

I
The Child, the Teacher, and Conflict as Gift and Challenge

1

The Beauty of Conflict

The first time I visited Italy, I was struck by how people there seemed to enjoy arguing. With animated voices and hands, and sometimes with everyone talking at once, their disagreements were lively and loud but seemed amiable. No one appeared hurt, no one withdrew, and no one flung threats of bodily harm. The dialogue was intense, but the emotion was positive. The feeling was akin to how one might feel about being witness to conflict in a story. All good stories contain some conflict: protagonist vs. antagonist, death vs. redemption, danger vs. safety, good vs. evil, and tension that ends with release. To a large degree, we relate to stories *because* of the conflict. We enjoy the hero's journey (Campbell, 1949), the battles, the victory, and the homecoming. Conflict along the way has changed the hero for the better, and he returns home with gifts for the world he once left. In appreciating the hero's story in books and films, we recognize conflict as necessary and worthwhile. Yet our associations with conflict in real life are rarely so positive.

When you think of "conflict," what are the first words that come to mind? Take a minute to write them down. Now read them out loud. How do you feel? Do those words have positive or negative connotations for you? Did your list contain words like "disagreement," "violence," "fighting," "hostility," or "clash?" Do those words feel good to say or a little bit yucky? Most of us have learned that conflict doesn't feel good. Some people feel the need to gird their loins before wading into conflict with uncharacteristic assertiveness. Others avoid conflict altogether. Each of us will have a different association with the concept, but the general emotion is often negative.

Even though we don't tend to think about conflict as a good thing, somehow our society has cultured it, supported by politics and leaders' intention to divide. It can be loud and messy and dividing. No one likes the feeling of being in conflict with others or oneself; we may put personal and professional dilemmas on the shelf in order to avoid grappling with disagreement, confusion, disequilibrium, or uncertainty. Or we may confront. Neither is likely to leave us satisfied. When teachers of young children consider conflict, they may think of children offending other children, of tears, and of management struggles. But conflict can be a gift for teachers and learners alike. In the leprechaun vignette, children accustomed to solving problems collaboratively showed us how disagreement can initiate dialogue and inspire problem-solving. Their teachers used the protocols in this book to help them confront conflict in a way that kept it cerebral and light, without the negative emotion that can shut negotiation down.

When we learn to have cognitive conflict without letting it overwhelm us emotionally or send us running back to those who think as we do, we can stay in the space where disagreements happen, and we can sit with uncertainty without a hit to our identity. If we recognize the many types of conflict that arise in teaching and learning and embrace positive conflict as a challenge to grow, we need not feel threatened when conflict in the classroom arises. We might encounter, for example:

- Cognitive conflict – when theories collide in research, conversation, or play. Confronto resides here.
- Social conflict – among children or among adults.
- Uncertainty – when teachers can't predict what's going to happen in the course of children's research.
- Disequilibrium – when old understandings are no longer satisfying in the light of new information.
- Sticking points in children's research and/or representation.

With a broadened understanding of the nature of conflict, we can think about problems, disagreements, uncertainty, and challenges as learning opportunities for all.

Conflict, either internal or external (or both), is necessary for change to occur. No learning happens without internal conflict in the form of disequilibrium or dissatisfaction with explanations that used to satisfy us. Our intelligence grows when we encounter ideas that conflict with our ideas. When decisions must be made, we can use conflict to help us analyze the problem. In the words of Dale Feinaurer (2017), conflict helps us avoid groupthink. If everyone in a community tacitly agrees to agree no matter what, simply to avoid facing opinions different from their own, assumptions are not examined, questions are not asked, decisions are poorly formed, and people can't grow.

At my daughter's first kindergarten parent-teacher conference, the teacher told me that she was doing well in general, but there was one thing she needed to work on. She told me that whenever there was a point of conflict, my child felt the need to continue to work on the problem until it was resolved. "Yes, and?" I responded. This is what we had taught her: you have a voice, and you have ears, and you can use them to negotiate until everyone involved is satisfied. "Well, it's a problem," the teacher told me. Here was an individual who abhorred conflict in her classroom and got out of it in the quickest way possible, which was to tell the children who was right and who was wrong and mete out punishment accordingly. My daughter's complaint: "They don't let us cry in kindergarten." She was stuck between one constraint and another. But her teacher was also stuck without an appreciation for the possibilities using conflict for good might offer.

The truth is that conflict, both interpersonal and intrapersonal, is inevitable. It's a far broader phenomenon than can be defined as "winning" or "losing," with more nuance and greater influence. It is a part of life. It is a challenge; it is an opportunity. It creates the possibility for change. It can lead to a shift in our perception of something. It can precipitate understanding of other people. It is a catalyst for growth. Our differences may create conflict that can lead to understanding and empathy.

Conflict makes us aware when something isn't right or isn't working. Conflict can contribute to the awakening of mind. If creativity is the capacity to make something new, conflict can be the spark.

We can learn how to use conflict as an asset in our teaching. Teachers who participate in children's research find that they must navigate sticking points particular to their work. Jumping into research with children can feel risky. There are moments when you may not know where an investigation is going. A project may stall. Social conflict may disrupt collaboration. You might feel uncertain in the face of conflict in the classroom, in your pedagogy, or in your research with children. Uncertainty is more evident in teaching this way than it is in a more traditional approach. I say "evident" because teachers' manuals and scripted curricula represent certainty to many teachers, but it's a bit misleading. You may be certain about what *you* plan to do, but you cannot be certain, ever, about what children will think or learn in response. For those engaging in research with children, this ... children's unique response to provocations[1] ... is where joy resides. Internal and external conflicts are inevitable when people are acting as themselves in uncontrived situations. If teachers who set out to join children in their research about the world view conflict as unsafe and do everything in their power to avoid good conflict, they will miss many opportunities to engage fully in the natural process of children's research. They may be tempted to resort to what they've always done or go on automatic pilot, even though they suspect that there is a better way. Teachers who are committed to the deep engagement and pleasure (for children and teachers) that participating in research with children brings might wish for an alternative to one-size-fits-all responses to conflict. They might wish for support that honors them as creative, thinking teachers and that shows them a way to *use* conflict in their teaching. The flexible protocols in this book are meant to support a new generation of teacher-researchers. They can be the teacher's coach, in a way, a teacher's teacher for times when she experiences conflict and doesn't know how to proceed.

Note

1. A provocation is an invitation to explore. It introduces something new for the children's consideration. It might be an object in the environment, an event, a question, or anything "provocative" enough to pique the imagination, make children ponder, and challenge the intellect. For more about provocations, see Chapters 8 and 10.

References

Campbell, J. (1949). *The Hero with a Thousand Faces* (1st ed.). Princeton University Press.

Feinaurer, D. (January 4, 2017). Why Conflict is a Good Thing. TEDx Oshkosh. https://youtu.be/TF38pGE7GBg

2
Who Is the Child?

Our image of the child (and, I will propose going forward, the teacher) is central to any flexible approach to teaching and learning. The educators of Reggio Emilia have taught us to ask, "Who is the child?" Do we see children as "cute" and fill the environment with cartoon characters and adorable decorations? As empty buckets or blank slates, we need to fill with "knowledge?" As "difficult" or naughty when they don't behave as expected? Notice the focus on the adult here. These beliefs create an image of the child for the beholder in which the child is considered an accessory or a bother to the adult. These values diminish the child. Our beliefs about children, learning, and teaching inform all our interactions with children and how we go about educating them. If we believe that children are blank slates waiting for us to write on them or empty vessels waiting for us to fill them, our pedagogy will consist of actions to impart information and "manage" the children. If we consider children accessories to our power in the classroom, our expectations will be weak, and the children are not likely to disappoint or surprise us.

Instead, if we believe that children are competent, intelligent, resourceful, and active seekers of relationships with other people and with the world around them, we will understand that there is nothing empty about a child. We will see the child not as an accessory but as a citizen of the world with rights and agency from the beginning of her life. We will listen to the children not only with our senses but also with curiosity. Our pedagogical decisions will be based on our understanding that the child is very much a protagonist in her own learning. We won't do for the child what he can do for himself. We will offer support, but not more than needed for the child to realize his intent. We will expect the child to be capable of having big ideas. We will strive to learn as much as we can about the children in front of us. We expect to be amazed at their brilliance, resourcefulness, and compassion…and we are.

A teacher who holds a strong image of the child tends to see the disconnect between what she knows about children and someone else's plans for her learning community. She would find the old scripts, which might have satisfied her if she thought of children as empty vessels, are no longer effective or appealing. She might also be wondering how to proceed in the face of sticking points (points of conflict) while honoring her beliefs about children, teaching, and learning. More on that to come.

> When teachers intuitively disregard a child's contribution to educational environments, they may be assuming the image of the child as an empty vessel to be filled with knowledge that is predetermined and fixed by the teacher. To take children's questions, activity, and expressions seriously as valid points of departure for future learning opportunities is to challenge this image of the child and to take the child seriously as a competent and capable learner. When teachers challenge this deficit image of the child, they assume another image – the child as the creator of culture and their own learning trajectories.
> Daniel Whitaker (2020)

What Do We Hope for Children and the World They Live In?

Our image of the child informs our hopes for him and the world he lives in. It is every child's right to learn in an environment that piques their curiosity and has myriad possibilities for relationships. We can create such an environment and hope that the world they find themselves in beyond the classroom will also invite their innovation and inquiry. We can hope that their world will want to hear what they have to say and that they will know how to say it. We can hope their world will not only challenge them but welcome the challenges they create. We can hope they will love learning so much that they choose it for the rest of their lives. We can make all these things happen for children in school in hopes that they will make them happen for themselves when they experience life outside of school. To take advantage of this world we want for the children, they will need to develop a set of dispositions and habits of mind that endure beyond this one year of school, beyond even school itself. By focusing on these goals, we might telescope learning from discrete subjects and an adult's idea of education as only what the child needs to know to what the child wants to *be*. We can differentiate education from schooling, where schooling is narrow in scope, but education is an umbrella over one's entire life. What a rich life it can be when learning becomes life and life becomes learning!

What do we want for the children we teach? Are we training good factory workers as the schooling system aimed to do in the 19th century? Or are we educating the people who will work together to solve the world's problems now and in the future? Will we be satisfied with a society whose citizens do not choose to read and cannot recognize that they are being misled and manipulated by social media or politicians? Or do we want to educate a populace who can think critically and are open to the perspectives of others? Do we want education to privilege a "me first" mindset, or do we want children to see themselves as integral to the community in which they live? When our current society has produced huge numbers of teenagers with serious mental health issues, what can educators do to bring purpose and joy back to school? From the bird's eye view of what we want for children, we can derive certain dispositions and habits of mind to get us there: a big idea curriculum, as it were. Consider what could happen if we are successful in helping children

- ♦ Develop awake minds
- ♦ Pay attention to their own curiosity and have the disposition to follow it

Who Is the Child? ◆ 21

- Develop a disposition toward inquiry
- Experience pleasure in learning
- Feel a desire to communicate and act on that desire
- Reach for relationships and know how to sustain them
- Challenge themselves
- Develop cognitive and emotional flexibility

More about each of these dispositions and habits of mind follows.

Develop Awake Minds

In the natural course of living, the youngest children tend to interact with the environment in an intuitive manner. They are not likely to plan; they just do. Even as they become preschoolers, they may not be fully aware of what they are doing and why. Do you remember doing something naughty as a child and only becoming aware that you did it when you were interrupted? I do. At 5 and the oldest of 4 children, I conscripted my siblings to create a skating rink in my parents' bedroom by covering the hardwood floor with baby powder and sliding around in stocking feet, which we did with joy. When our mother came into the room, aghast, I remember "waking up" as if from a dream, aware for the first time that I hadn't *planned* this delinquency, but when interrupted, I just found myself having done it. It was enough of a revelation that I still remember it, the "waking up" more than the actual activity. There was no punishment; my mother says she had to leave the room so we wouldn't see her laughing, and I suppose she had us help clean up the mess. My emotional memory (as so many memories from early childhood are) must have been about the "waking up" moment of that adventure. As children grow, so does executive function, and they become more aware of their process. Eventually, this awareness allows them to plan, follow through, and evaluate their decisions. Only then can their actions be assumed to be premeditated. Frequently at the beginning of a school year, I would observe a child who, a minute ago, was playing happily at the block area just get up and leave. If I asked, "Are you finished playing with blocks?" it was not unusual for the child to seem to "wake up" and say, "Oh. No, I'm not!!" and go back to playing there. Watch the movement of the children in your class. Do they seem to be aware of their transitions? Do they have a plan in mind? How can we support their growing executive function? How can we elicit awake minds?

Pay Attention to Their Own Curiosity and Have the Disposition to Follow It; Develop a Disposition toward Inquiry

Children are born researchers. No one has to teach them how to be curious or engage in inquiry about the world. Rather, schooling often teaches them *not* to follow their curiosity. To conform. To answer questions more than they ask them. To look for what the teacher wants. To seek validation from adults by giving the right answer. How can we safeguard children's curiosity and make space for increasingly sophisticated inquiry? How can thinking teachers support thinking children?

Experience Pleasure in Learning

Again, this is not something that must be learned. As my infant granddaughter investigates a new object or phenomenon, I hear her expressing pleasure with giggles, chortles, and exclamations. Babies choose to explore, experiment, and study everything. No one has to assign them a task. This is the natural state. There is immense pleasure in learning when it happens without a hit to self-confidence and a sense of agency. The child who experiences joy in discovery, competence, and problem-solving will seek it out. But it is not impenetrable. So often I have watched children lose their joy in learning at school slowly, slowly. Does anyone intend for this to happen? Of course not. But it is created, nonetheless.

Feel a Desire to Communicate and Act on that Desire

The desire to communicate is also innate. The three-month-old communicates by catching your eye and smiling. She has learned that people respond when she does that, and she wants that response. No one needs to teach her to *want* to communicate. We should want children to become as adept as possible at expressive and receptive language, right? But too often, school hinders the child's natural drive for expression by privileging the teacher's voice or forgetting/not knowing that expression comes in verbal, graphic, *and* temporal languages. As school is a social environment and communication requires other people, we have an opportunity to support increasingly sophisticated expressive and receptive communication that must not be squandered. Reading and writing are communication systems. How we teach literacy can foster children's sense of agency with language and take advantage of their natural drive to communicate. But if literacy instruction focuses on disparate skills over connection, we might compromise the forest (the drive to communicate) for the trees.

Reach for Relationship

Relationships with those who care for us and with those we care about are fundamental to our well-being. There's a case to be made that relationships and a sense of belonging drive most of our social decisions, children and adults alike. As educators, we reach for ways to develop our relationship with the children in our care and help them navigate the social terrain of their lives. We can set up the classroom environment to enable the children to pursue their intent to collaborate. We can develop communication systems to foster the relationship between families and the school. We can support children's efforts both to articulate their needs and wants and to build, sustain, and repair relationships with peers.

Challenge Themselves

Every year I delighted in witnessing the growth of those children who entered my class unwilling to accept a challenge, let alone challenge themselves to do new things. As their confidence grew during the year, they started to challenge themselves. Once they experienced the pleasure of creating their own challenges, they expanded the kinds of tasks they took on. Often, the first challenges were physical: "Watch me walk on this wall!" In time, the challenges became more cognitive. Confidence and Challenge grew alongside each other.

Children will challenge themselves naturally if it feels safe to do so. Crawling babies will pull themselves up on the coffee table. They will figure out how to sit back down without falling hard. And then they will stand, sit, stand, sit, stand, sit, creating and accepting the challenge all by themselves. Some are more sensitive to discouragement (from adults, peers, or past failures) than others. What happened to the five-year-olds who are afraid to try? How do we get in the way? We can penalize mistakes instead of celebrating them as our teachers. We can send the message that the child is not safe and make her question her competence by constantly saying, "Be careful" or otherwise warning children off challenging/risky endeavors. We need alternatives to those responses if we want children to assess and take risks, with their bodies and their minds. If all the challenges at school are conceived, curated, and evaluated by adults, the natural inclination of the infant and toddler to challenge themselves may wither.

Develop Cognitive and Emotional Flexibility

It takes flexibility to think outside the box when facing problems; to consider the ideas of another and weigh them against your own; to negotiate in the face of social conflict; to consider a plan B; to think creatively; to face the blank page; to tolerate transitions well; and to feel OK about having to change gears when things don't go as expected. What can teachers do to foster flexibility?

Not all the children in my school went to Junior Kindergarten with us. The kindergarten teachers in my school told me they often referred moments of conflict to the JK alumnae in their classes because they could always come up with a plan B. In one such story, a group of children had spent a great deal of time building a structure with blocks. For some reason, the structure had to be dismantled, and the children were distressed. The teacher didn't quite know what to do with the children's emotions. A JK alum swooped in and said, "That's OK. We can just draw the [building] so we can remember how to build it again." That satisfied everyone, and the children were able to take the structure apart.

All the dispositions above are either present when a child is born or develop naturally as he explores his world at the beginning of his life. Our first job as caring adults is to safeguard them. Sometimes school does the opposite for the sake of management and compliance. In addition to making sure these innate dispositions survive, we must also support children's use of the dispositions to develop concomitant habits of mind. For example, the children come to us reaching for relationships. We can help them develop the language they need to form and sustain relationships. We can help them grow their social courage, find their voice, learn to listen and respond to the ideas of others, and learn strategies for solving social problems while maintaining their drive to form and grow relationships. Unlike learning new facts, which can slip off the mental desktop all too quickly, sustaining original dispositions and growing concomitant habits of mind stay with a child and can serve him for his whole life. Those dispositions and habits of mind can create the lifelong learner, the autodidact, and the individual who searches actively for meaning.

The effects of a curriculum based on what we hope for children long-term can be lasting and profound. I recently attended a high school graduation party for former Junior Kindergarten students and their parents. The graduates remembered specific research projects from 13 years earlier (one attributed her decision to pursue science in college to an investigation in which she had participated in JK!), but the parents marveled about the way the students had continued to use the dispositions and habits of mind that they grew all that time ago, despite the fact that no future school experience directly addressed any of it. After JK, their education was primarily traditional, often delivered with a deficit mindset.

It is our responsibility to ensure children will experience a world that invites engagement with all the dispositions and habits of mind mentioned above. This world is the right of every child. The adults in a child's life have everything to do with the possibility of this world for them, including teachers who manifest exactly those characteristics we hope that children will develop: awake minds to notice opportunities to support children's learning; curiosity as teacher-researchers; a hunger for learning; the desire and ability to communicate and collaborate with everyone in the learning triad (child, teacher, family); the disposition to challenge themselves. The adults in a child's life must decide whether to privilege compliance or creativity, and they must figure out how to act on their choice.

Reference

Whitaker, D. (2020, March 17). *The Image of the Child.* https://theeducationhub.org.nz/the-image-of-the-child/

3

Who Is the Teacher?

Teachers have the right to deep engagement, just as children do. The image of the teacher held by administrators, pedagogical support professionals, and teachers themselves *is as important to children's learning as the teacher's image of the child*. We are accustomed to claiming such things for children, but in too many settings, this is not how the education system treats teachers or how teachers think of themselves.

When I was a fledgling teacher and starting to innovate on the archaic kindergarten curriculum I had inherited, an older, more experienced teacher warned me that a teacher could never know what children needed to learn and that I should make sure that whatever I did came from a published teacher's manual. Born a thinker, I chewed on that piece of advice like a hunk of gristle. It never did sit right. Now I understand that that individual held a limited image of the teacher (herself included) and operated under a veil of insecurity. Then and now, in the traditional school world, those who are not in the classroom and do not know its children are empowered to ascertain what children should know and when, in whole blocks and in adult time. School systems mandate "teacher-proof" curricula, often designed to prepare children for the next grade. In an interview with Lella Gandini, Loris Malaguzzi "compared a school that privileges readiness for primary school as a funnel. He said, 'then we educators are… prisoners of a model that acts like a funnel. I think, moreover, that the funnel is a detestable object, and it is not much appreciated by children either. Its purpose is to narrow down what is big into what is small'" (Gandini, 2012). In contrast, we want to accompany and support children as they take the germ of an idea and grow it large.

Teachers in too many schools work in a culture of coercion and are reluctant to innovate for fear of reprisal. But most teachers have so much more to offer than compliance! They and onsite leaders are, in fact, the *only* ones who can know what the children in their classes really need. Teachers in too many contexts have had their sense of agency taken away. Their own safety becomes primary for those teachers. There is just so much innovation allowed, and the safest kind is the most superficial kind, so teachers may express their creativity with artful bulletin boards or ancillary curriculum add-ons. In time, creative thinking gets boxed. Teachers learn to rely on scripts and tricks. Even if given the opportunity to make teaching and learning decisions on their own and with colleagues, they may be afraid to. Their image of themselves is small compared to their capabilities. Somehow, educators must set themselves free from a limited and limiting image of the teacher. They must come to expect that their role as educators can reflect their intelligence, creativity, and cognitive flexibility. School and district leaders have a primary role in redefining teaching, learning, and expectations for educators. Until that happens, let teachers become awake to the ways in which the education system defines them as direction-followers and box tickers. Let them look within for another way.

The Thinking Teacher

The teacher-researchers in the preprimary schools of Reggio Emilia (i.e. all the teachers) study children, learning, and teaching through action research. Action research is both investigative and functional. The reflective teacher-researcher identifies real and significant questions about children and learning at the same time as he changes his practice to reflect what the research has revealed. He is an investigator of children, with children. He is a thinking teacher: more than a manager of an inherited curriculum, more than so many teachers have been led to believe they are.

When thinking teachers observe expressions that they do not expect in children's play, conversation, and representation, they ask *why*. What are the children thinking? What are they trying to figure out? They study, hypothesize, theorize, and practice based on the theories of great educational philosophers (for example, John Dewey, Piaget, Vygotsky, Howard Gardner, Jerome Bruner, and Loris Malaguzzi), but they also construct their own theories about children, teaching, and learning. This is not a linear process but a cyclical one: from question to observation to provisional theory to investigation, which leads to more questions, and so on. In this way, the teacher-researcher solves problems creatively, is always seeking to learn about the children in front of him, and, by making his research public, adds to the global knowledge base about children and learning. To do this, teachers must see themselves as intelligent, resourceful, creative, capable of interpreting the meaning of children's play, representation, and communication, and capable of much more than following directions. The teacher in the Reggio-inspired classroom understands that he is there to learn from the children how to support their research.

A stance of curiosity leads the thinking teacher to listen more than she talks. Listening gives her access to the children's thinking in a way that presenting information in a traditional style never could. She is also an active participant in the children's research. She works to recognize the children's intent (the meaning they are trying to make) and to support their efforts to realize that intent. She is not satisfied with the limitations of scripts and canned curricula. She is reluctant to operate "the way we always did it" without examination of assumptions and practices. *Why* have we always done it that way? Is it really in service to our image of the child and our beliefs of what education should be? The thinking teacher might look at old scripts from a bird's eye view and ask, "What's being learned here?" and try to answer honestly. She pays attention to the children, engages in intelligent listening, expects to be amazed at what she observes, and focuses on the children's agenda and not just her own. She does not try, nor does she accept, a separation between theory and practice. Rather, she knows that they are reciprocal. The schools of Reggio Emilia are considered "the place theory and practice touch like the magic moment when night becomes day" (Braedekamp, 2008), and the thinking teacher knows one cannot exist without the other.

Acting on one's identity as a teacher-researcher takes a certain courage, especially in the current educational climate. The teacher who is confident in his ability to listen and observe and who is willing to work to understand what children are trying to mean in their play, conversation, and representation will be able to muster the courage teaching on the edge requires. How does that confidence develop? As far as I know, the only way is through. That is, we study children and learning by listening with curiosity and an intent to understand, by making mistakes and trying again, and by documenting our own process along with that of the children. We cultivate our ability to articulate why we are doing what we are doing, i.e., the values behind our work and our observations of the children's intellectual and personal growth. We document and share the learning stories from our classrooms. With documentation and theory behind us, we can be more confident in stepping into children's research with them.

Research with Children

Children's research is the curriculum of the thinking teacher's classroom. Children ask, "How does life work?" Their action in response is their research. The teacher's job is to support that research with materials, tools, challenging questions, documentation, and her own curiosity for as long as the investigation lasts. Teacher-researchers cultivate an "attitude of research" (Rinaldi, 2006) in the classroom: research of, for, and with the children. In schools where this is not the case, children are greeted with a curriculum that asks them to put away their curiosity and natural inclination to investigate. Much is lost unless we choose to build upon children's innate curiosity, keen intellect, and creativity. So deep is the learning and so great are the personal resources that children develop through engaging in research that the choice between the two schools becomes an ethical one. If we know how much greater the learning is with one approach over the other, is it right to make school all about compliance and rote learning?

One way to connect our values (what we hope for children and the world they live in) to our practice is to engage in children's research alongside them. We know that the moment they are born, children begin to experiment to figure out the world they are in. We can see it in the newborn looking for a face, the infant putting everything in his mouth, or the toddler heading for the dog's water bowl but stopping to turn and look at you…will you tell him no? We don't have to teach children to engage in research. But educators do have a vital role. First, we are responsible for keeping the environment conducive to research, including interactions with adults and time given over to exploration. Collaborative inquiry can yield even greater rewards than individual research, and it is up to the teacher to support children as they learn how to engage in research together. As she does, she can accompany the children artfully, knowing when to get out of the way, knowing when and how to offer support, acting as memory keeper and documenter, and doing her own action research.

In a Reggio-inspired classroom, you will see groups of children engaging in a research project based on an idea or question that has great meaning to those children. A research project (aka "investigation" or "project") will start with a question or a problem originating from one child's passion, a common interest, a naturally occurring event, or a question the teacher poses based on her curiosity about the children and their thinking. The teacher supports the children's efforts to make meaning of the topic they are investigating. A research project may last a day, or it might last most of a year. The teacher encourages deep engagement, and the end comes only when the children are satisfied. Later in the book, you will find the stories of some research projects with four- and five-year-olds that illustrate how such investigations might go. As you read them, you will see how the children's research and the teacher's research intersect, creating a research lab of sorts in the early childhood classroom.

Consider This

- What is your image of the child? How does your practice reflect that image?
- What is your image of yourself as a teacher? What do you wish it to be? These are good questions to bring to a meeting with colleagues. Can you ask a colleague to observe your classroom and notice where your practice follows your stated image of the child and where it doesn't?

References

Bredekamp, S. (2008). "Malaguzzi's Metaphors: The Power of Imagery to Transform Educational Practice and Policy" in Gandini, L., Etheredge, S., & Hill, L., eds. *Insights and Inspirations from Reggio Emilia: Stories of Teachers and Children from North America*. Davis. 49.

Gandini, L. (2012). "History, Ideas, and Basic Principles: An Interview With Loris Malaguzzi" in Edwards, C., Gandini, L., & Forman, G. (Eds.), *The Hundred Languages of Children: The Reggio Emilia Experience in Transformation* (3rd ed.). Praeger. 49.

Rinaldi, C. (2006). *In Dialogue with Reggio Emilia, Listening, Researching and Learning*. Routledge. 101.

4

The Role of Inner and External Conflict in Teaching and Learning

Inner Conflict for the Learner

Conflict plays an important role in the learning process. Without certain types of conflict, there is no change, no growth, no learning. For example, cognitive dissonance or disequilibrium, a type of inner conflict, is the state in which new information challenges our current understanding. It is how our understanding becomes more sophisticated and nuanced. When we encounter an unfamiliar phenomenon, one that our current cognitive schema can't explain, we may take that new information and, with it, construct a new, more complete understanding.

Three-year-old Matteo has a pet dog. He knows that dogs are animals with 4 legs; they stand horizontally, have fur, and they bark. One day he goes for a ride in the country with his mom. They pass a cow pasture with a few cattle lingering by the roadside fence. Matteo studies the big animals a bit. His mother pulls the car over and opens the window so Matteo can have a better look. His brain says: Animal…check. Four legs…check. Horizontal…check. Fur…check. "Dog!" he exclaims. Suddenly, one cow moos. That is not a bark! We might think about the place in Matteo's brain where the characteristics Matteo has assigned to his pet reside as a mental "box" defined as "dog." But this animal no longer fits into the dog "box" in his mind. He needs to construct a new box within the animal category in his brain.

"No, honey, that's a cow," his mother says thereby adding to Matteo's disequilibrium, upon which he will act. If the new information is too far from his current understanding, he may ignore it. But if Matteo accommodates the new information, he will have two cognitive "boxes," dog and cow, where there once was one.

Matteo experienced the conflict of disequilibrium between the assumption (dog) and the new information (moo). It can be an uncomfortable state, and that discomfort pushes us forward to construct a new understanding. So, though it can feel unsettled and uncomfortable, it's how we learn. Children seem to tolerate this inner conflict better than many adults. They are just learning about the world and how it works, and every day is likely to contain some moments of disequilibrium. They countenance disequilibrium without the fear and shame of being wrong that is likely to result when school (and to some degree, life) privileges the right answer over exploration and experimentation. They have not yet learned that being right can become something to protect at all costs, and it is up to us to make sure they don't. Curiosity is a casualty of the need to be right. In so many ways, we teach children to value correctness over curiosity, over trial and error, over innovation. Herein lies a common conflict between our values and our practice. If we want to encourage children to take the risks most conducive to learning, we may need to learn a new language in responding to our toddlers', preschoolers', and older students' efforts to learn. Will we continue to applaud only correct attempts? Or also celebrate children's mistakes as a path to learning? What does that look like in the early childhood classroom?

Although we all learn by taking information and acting on it some way to construct knowledge, we glean another benefit from co-constructing knowledge in good conflict with others. The educators in Reggio Emilia, inspired by the theories of Lev Vygotsky, have described this special benefit of working with diverse perspectives. According to Carlina Rinaldi, "Controversy and the conflict of ideas play a fundamental role...bringing out the significant aspects of individual thought and at the same time giving new meaning to the knowledge-building process"

(2006). Each individual in a group brings her own experiences, knowledge, and opinions to the others. Together, the children co-construct new understandings that would not have been possible without the interaction and conflicting views of the others. In this way, the group develops its own intelligence, which is distinct from the intelligence of each of its members. So, in a group of five, there are six intelligences: one for each child and a sixth for the group.

In addition, encountering conflicting ideas in play or research allows children to practice articulating their point of view, having cognitive conflict without emotional flooding, listening to the perspectives of others, and negotiating. The greater the diversity of perspective in a group, the greater the possibility for cognitive conflict among its members, and that enriches everyone.

I've been writing about children here. But the title of this subchapter is Inner and External Conflict for *the learner*. These things are true for all learners, children, and adults alike.

Inner and External Conflict for Teachers

At times, facing inner conflict is a courageous act. Jen worked as a reading teacher at a Title One public school. Her children had been in my junior kindergarten class, and she had studied the blog posts I published every day as part of my action research. When she got the opportunity to change roles and teach kindergarten at her school for the first time, she wondered if she could bring the Reggio principles that so resonated with her and her daughters to her new classroom. I agreed to be her pedagogical companion/consultant as she made this courageous change. This was the first of a series of conflict-rich opportunities she encountered in her new position. First, she was about to tackle two new things simultaneously: a different teaching and learning paradigm and a grade level she hadn't taught before. Second, she was accustomed to being an expert in her field. Now she was choosing to put herself in a vulnerable position, a position of not knowing, in order to accomplish her goal. We worked together for three years, navigating and negotiating a path toward inquiry-based pedagogy in a public school where teacher compliance was privileged. We encountered sticking points particular to the juxtaposition of standards-based curriculum and inquiry-based practice. More teachers joined the program each year. Cognitive conflict among colleagues and external conflict with schedules and requirements emerged. We had to be clear about the values behind our choices...why we were doing what we were doing... and transparent about the learning we saw.

In an effort toward that transparency, we encouraged the children to turn toward the rest of the school whenever we had a chance. One day, two kindergarten girls hatched a plan to have a sleepover at school. When Jen told them they'd have to get approval from the principal to do that, the girls decided to write a letter to the principal. In their letter asking for permission, they invited the principal to come and bring her "husbin" and asked for a reply. The principal wrote back, saying she would let them know when she decided. This inspired the girls to try harder. They decided to write a more specific letter back, this time on such big paper that, they figured, the principal could not ignore it. This time, they asked if the principal would not only allow the sleepover but also bring bacon and a dog. And so, this exchange continued. No sleepover occurred. But it didn't seem to matter to the girls in the end. The questions, the letters, and the connection were the project.

Knowing that the girls were learning through the process (literacy concepts, yes, but also about their power to make things happen), Jen reached through the unease of engaging in this endeavor. I was there to support her, but the heavy lifting was hers. She had many moments of uncertainty when wondering whether and how much to help the girls, how to help them sustain their engagement (it turns out all they needed was time, materials, and space), and a feeling of vulnerability when making transparent to others in the school what she was doing that was not in the prescribed curriculum or compliant with the sanctioned schedule. The children's intellectual, academic, and personal growth and the joy Jen experienced during this project made working through the uncertainty worthwhile.

A child copies the word "Sincerely" from the principal's letter about the girls' proposal for a sleepover at school.

Adults seem to find disequilibrium and other types of internal conflict less tolerable than children do. We tend to specialize as we mature and stay within our intellectual comfort zone. We may stick with people who think like we do, and whose living circumstances correspond to ours. We may not choose to take the risk of trying new things. But the rewards can be tremendous if we do "put ourselves out there," follow our curiosity about the children we work with, and consider a brave new paradigm to replace a tired old one or one that no longer makes sense for today's children and tomorrow's world. It can make us feel alive, awake, and energized. We can learn to sit with uncertainty if we trust that the children will eventually engage in meaningful research. We can let the children be our teachers by changing our lens when we are observing. We can find commonalities with unlikely colleagues and become better at articulating our values and theories. We can let internal conflict invite us into deeper understanding of teaching and learning.

How do we learn to embrace uncertainty, tolerate and even seek out the unknown, take risks, and see the beauty in inner and external conflict? Will it help to shift our perspective and embrace the possibilities that would *not* be possibilities if we ran from inner conflict? To form learning communities among ourselves? To seek out pedagogical companions (Pelo & Carter, 2018) and come to understand that we are not alone? To have a *plan* for the inevitable uncertainty and sticking points in our work with children and each other?

Teachers experience inner conflict when they don't quite know how to proceed but don't want to resort to "what we've always done" just because it's always been done. It happens when a teacher observes a child who upends her current understanding of how children learn. I remember such a moment in my first year of teaching kindergarten. New to teaching, I listened to more experienced teachers and the reading program's teacher's manual. I was supposed to be controlling the text my kindergarteners were trying to read. One day 5-year-old Mary brought a book to school and declared that she could read it and asked me to help her. It was a nonfiction book for which my current understanding said she was not ready. I was in conflict. This wasn't part of the plan, but I couldn't bring myself to discourage her. So, we sat down together to read it. She needed support as she read, but she did it. I realized that she learned a lot about how readers solve problems in that session, and her pride at her accomplishment was palpable. I sat with my discomfort in the fight between what I "knew" and the new situation that Mary presented long enough to move through disequilibrium, give "breaking the rules" a try, and I learned something. That was the day I recognized the power of motivation and determination to transcend limitations in learning. It was also the day I discovered the value of examining the rules. I was very young, and the example is simple, but my experience with Mary that day was formative for me. As inner conflict, disequilibrium is essential for learning, and teachers are learners in their classrooms as much as children are. Do you remember a specific moment of inner conflict that resulted in a new understanding? What was your response to the discomfort? If you have an awake mind, if you are of the mindset that the children will teach you much if you really listen, you may be gifted frequent bouts of disequilibrium and its subsequent growth.

The Inner Conflict of Uncertainty

We have become a dichotomized society. This or that, right or left, in or out. As a society, we seem to have lost our collective flexibility of mind and heart. Perhaps that is what makes us cling to certainty so mightily. This is not new; it has just been magnified in recent years. It has become imperative that we find ways to educate a new generation of children who can think flexibly, engage in cognitive conflict without emotional conflict, hold onto the curiosity with which they are born, and value relationships with other people and ideas over empty and depleting technological "rabbit holes." It is also essential that we adults become these things: flexible, curious, responsive, thinking teachers who can use conflict for good.

In classrooms where children's research is honored, and teachers work to support it, uncertainty in the research trajectory is inevitable. If we are truly collaborators with children instead of directors of their research, we can expect that

- ♦ There will be times when we are not certain where the research is going, or even if it's going anywhere at all.
- ♦ We may wonder when, if ever, the children will engage in a rich research project.
- ♦ We may not know how to help the children continue their forward motion around a topic.

This uncertainty is both uncomfortable and universal. It is part of the process of doing research with children. We must trust that we can navigate the waves of uncertainty and that they will give way to beautiful things.

Shame in "Failure"

Shame can act like brakes in the learning process for teachers, too. It can cause an overwhelming emotional state, and no one can think in the face of emotional overload. It can block access to curiosity or even make it feel dangerous. As such, it represents conflict between what we value/want to do and what we are able to do.

To disempower shame when things don't go the way we hoped they would in the classroom, we need a new framework and a new understanding of the process of supporting children's research. If we can understand failure as just one of our "teachers," perhaps we can fade out our tendency toward shame. This is easier to say than to accomplish. I know that I tend to remember my failures far longer than I remember my successes, and I suspect it has to do with my own education at home and at school. I can't negate past experiences. But I can control my response. Like any strong emotion, shame can sometimes be mitigated with a cognitive overlay. That is, reminding myself what a particular failure taught me does help to alleviate the paralysis that shame in failure can produce.

Conflict Around Values, Practice, and Expectations

In my role as a pedagogical consultant, I like to meet with teachers and/or administrators before I go into their classrooms to get a sense of what they are thinking, where their values about teaching and learning lie, and what their goals are. Sometimes what I hear them say about what they believe is not at all what I see when I go into the classrooms. It is in the classroom and not in our initial conversation that I truly learn about their image of the child. Teachers may tell me that they believe that children learn best when engaged with peers. Then I see that, in the classroom, everyone is working alone at a table, with the teacher walking around reminding the children to pay attention to their own work. Or a preschool teacher may tell me she values the power of choice, but in the classroom, children are cycled through centers on a schedule, with an emphasis on assuring every child works at every station over the course of a few days. The disconnect between stated beliefs and practice is conflict that makes growth for the teacher difficult. Her beliefs and her practice are severed. Of course, it's likely she isn't aware, and that's where she could use a pedagogical companion…peer, school leader, or consultant…to help her see the discrepancy. You can imagine that when she does become aware, there will be a certain level of emotional inner conflict, both over learning about the discrepancy and not yet knowing how to bridge the gap.

Sometimes, there is alignment between a teacher's values about teaching and learning and her knowledge about how to put them into practice, but conflict arises between those values and the school's or district's requirements. During the two and a half years I worked as a consultant to bring Reggio principles into the public school kindergarten, I was struck by how the teachers, who wanted to grow and innovate, were paralyzed by fear. I often heard "I don't dare" in response to a suggestion for even small changes. In a culture that discouraged risk-taking and strongly encouraged compliance, fear became a sticking point and a locus of inner conflict for the teachers. Even the daily schedule, set by a committee of administrators and divided into 20- or 30-minute chunks, could get in the way of the integrated practice they sought. There was no flexible protocol to address this particular area of conflict. Even if the kindergarten teachers in that school saw the children as competent, intelligent, and resourceful, the rest of the school did not, and the culture of coercion made resorting to old scripts the easiest path for those teachers. However, they did some serious creative problem-solving under the radar.

With the support of an amiable principal, those teachers embarked on some significant work during the first two and a half years of the project. Then, a new superintendent closed the windows the previous principal and superintendent had opened, and the project ended in its third year. But the kindergarten teachers left that experience more awake to the possibilities than when they started, and the kindergartners from those three years had life-changing experiences that parents reported extended far beyond the school's walls.

Most likely, we made the conflict between teachers' beliefs and requirements from the school system more evident to those who were paying attention. As the teachers gained a new understanding of what the children could do when they shifted their image of the children and offered opportunities for inquiry and creative thinking, the contrast between their beliefs and their previous practices became starker. This is the conflict that, at scale, could change education for the better.

Disagreements with Colleagues

We Americans have a tendency toward dichotomy. Our thinking may be boxed in by an unwillingness to consider shades of grey, even around complex issues. Without flexibility of mind, a society loses some of its range. Though the limitations of dichotomous thinking have dominated the public discourse lately, it does seem to be human nature to pick sides. When I was in my mid-20s and starting at a new school, I was aware that there had been some upheaval among faculty and administration the year before, but I didn't know what it was about. One day early in the year, a teacher approached me and said, "I do hope you'll be on our side." I never knew (or cared to know) what sides were involved, but this is the mindset that creates (and/or represents) "either/or" thinking and social conflict. It is limiting. Instead of acknowledging that we all wanted the same things for our students and looking for ways to find common ground, the faculty was expending energy on the emotions around conflict.

With that same group of colleagues, I discovered a disturbing trend that I called the "lounge effect." The teachers' lounge, where many gathered during their breaks, became a forum for complaining about children and families. Though I didn't spend much time in the lounge, I had to be there sometimes and was witness to what felt like a sort of unwritten compact to agree. Working on the assumption that children with challenges were challenge itself, the teachers complained, expecting the tacit agreement of the others. Looking back, I can see that what was missing in that lounge was conflict. If someone within the established group had challenged the silent compact that "everyone will agree with me," the teachers may have considered another perspective, for example, that children who are "challenging" are behaving with positive intent and it is our job to figure out what that intent is. Without anyone to challenge the unquestioned assumption, it persisted to the detriment of the children.

Conflict is growth, but we do have to work through it. Whether we agree with others or not, we can value the multiplicity of perspectives. We can know that different minds have the potential to enrich each other. Instead of oversimplifying the views of others as "their side," what if we were to look for where our views intersect, or almost do? For example, imagine that teachers of two different classes in the same school disagree about whether children should be made to wear their coats outdoors. The teachers know they have to have a consistent policy. One teacher wants it to be a rule, and the other wants the children to listen to their bodies and decide for themselves. Drill down into the issue, and you realize that both teachers want the children to have what they need to stay warm enough. That's the core of the issue. Since they don't disagree about the importance of self-determination for the children, perhaps they come to agree that they will ask the children to take their coats outside on a cool day if they don't want to wear them. Then, if they get cold, they can put them on.

If teachers have cultivated an expectation that disagreements can be catalysts for growth for all involved, they can approach disagreements with a strategy: look for the core of the issue and negotiate from there. Of course, there are conditions: the teachers must be cognitively and emotionally flexible. For that to happen, they need to feel safe within the group. In my opinion, school leaders have everything to do with creating a school culture where everyone feels safe to disagree and valued as creative and intelligent. In addition, leaders can hold up the value of conflict and negotiation to their faculty as worth the time and effort.

Consider This

What stories do you have about conflict:

- Internally. What was happening when you felt conflicted? What happened to resolve it? What did you learn?
- Social conflict. How are problems in your classroom solved? What is your role in the resolution? How did each of the participants in a moment of conflict feel after the problem was solved?
- Think of a time when you encountered conflict with a colleague. How was it resolved? How did you feel when it was over? How do you imagine the other person felt? How is your relationship now?

References

Pelo, A. & Carter, M. (2018). *From Teaching to Thinking: A Pedagogy for Reimagining Our Work*. Exchange Press.

Rinaldi, C. (2006). *In Dialogue with Reggio Emilia, Listening, Researching and Learning*. Routledge. 101.

Rinaldi, C. (2006). *In Dialogue with Reggio Emilia, Listening, Researching and Learning*. Routledge. 127.

5
Challenges to Pedagogical Flow

Children and teachers have the right to deep engagement in their work together. Without that deep engagement, we miss an opportunity to experience joy in teaching and learning. Imagine how inaccessible deep engagement might be in the school climate where teachers' schedules are set by others (or, following scripts and assumptions, by even the teachers themselves) to change gears every 20–30 minutes. Sometimes, the chopped-up day is even justified as necessary due to children's "short attention spans." This is one of those assumptions that, if examined, might be shown to be false. Young children can become absorbed for long periods if they are deeply engaged in the research they are doing or in play uninterrupted by conflict they cannot resolve. How can teachers realize their own right to deep engagement when they, too, must change gears every 20 minutes? I imagine that teachers who experience the joy of deep engagement would do anything to keep it.

How do teachers find deep engagement in the first place? Listening, a state of curiosity, and an expectation that you will be amazed by children's capacities are key to full engagement for the teacher. When things are going well…children are engaged in meaningful work, and the teacher is engaged with them or documenting children's process… everyone may experience what Mihaly Csikszentmihalyi calls "Flow" (1990), where you are so deeply immersed in what you are doing that nothing else registers and time passes unnoticed. Have you ever been so deeply engaged that when you finally look up hours after you began, it feels like only a minute has passed? That is Flow. Full engagement can lead to a lovely state of Flow. Csikszentmiyalyi also says that spending as much of your life as possible in a state of Flow is the key to happiness. Teachers and children have a right to that happiness in the classroom. It is not often articulated in curriculum documents, but shouldn't living a happy life be a primary goal in education? Japanese educator, Tsunesaburo Makiguchi, in response to an early 20th-century Japanese education system based on rote memorization and conformity, emphasized the need to find ways to foster students' love of learning. He believed that happiness should be the goal of education.

> Other than 'happiness' there is no word that fully and accurately expresses the unhindered pursuit of the cultural life that is the objective of education. From my own experience of the past several decades and from pondering this question over that time, I have come to believe this word gives the most realistic, straightforward and apt expression to the goal of life desired and sought by all people.
>
> (Makiguchi, 1930)

Here we are, almost a century later, and the stated goals in US district guidelines and practices are far from considering happiness as a goal in schools. Though everyone approves of fostering the love of learning, practices in many districts are counter to it. Deep engagement is requisite for experiencing both Flow and a sustained love of learning.

It seems to me that young children find Flow in play quite easily. You know that's where they've been when an interruption seems to wake them up from a dream. It can be elusive in school, though, if the environment and/or schedule doesn't support deep engagement. Flow can be interrupted by social conflict, difficulty doing something hard, or expectations that don't create the right conditions for deep engagement.

As a teacher I did not find Flow in the classroom until I began to engage in research with children and for children. Following scripts like those in teachers' manuals for each subject never allowed for it. In my first years as a teacher, I was constantly changing gears and focused on following directions written by someone who didn't know me or the children in my class. Finding Flow for me was a journey that involved setting up an environment in which children could find true and deep engagement; observing and creating traces of children's process in that environment (documenting); taking a listening stance; and approaching teaching in a true state of curiosity about children's thinking and about the topics that interest them. It involved expecting that the children would amaze me. And it required time to become truly and deeply engaged.

Even in the optimal environment, where a teacher is observing with a disposition toward curiosity, sticking points will emerge and prevent or interrupt Flow. Projects stall or conflict arises, and the teacher may feel at a loss for what to do. The coming chapters illustrate some of those sticking points and introduce the flexible protocols I have used to address them so that investigations and relationships can move beyond conflict and toward growth for children and teachers.

Points of Conflict

Points of conflict are obstacles that threaten to disrupt the flow of daily life in the classroom. For one reason or another, teachers and/or children get stuck in their negotiation of the work they do together. Social conflict disrupts play. Disequilibrium, in which we sit uncomfortably not knowing what to do, can paralyze us or cause us to disengage. Challenges to the rhythm of play and inquiry can make us worry, and they can derail research. Cognitive conflict can morph into emotional conflict. We may experience the yucky feeling of being stuck, of not knowing what to do. Points of conflict may tempt teachers to fall back on quick fixes and old scripts. No wonder teachers (and, perhaps especially, administrators) resort to codified scripts like teacher's manuals and how-to materials!

Participating in children's research can be one of the most rewarding ways to teach. It can put both teacher and children in the unique position of learning together. For me, it's what kept the process alive and joyful for decades. The flip side for the teacher who engages in research with children, however, is that they are likely to encounter a particular set of sticking points. A point of conflict may emerge when you don't see the potential for significant work in what the children are doing. Or the children suddenly lose interest in a topic you thought was compelling. Or social conflict disrupts play, relationships are wounded, and the children can't get back into their play. Perhaps the children are struggling with representing their ideas and you don't know how to help without taking over. Or disagreement in conversation threatens to end children's engagement. Perhaps the expectations of the school system don't match your values. Or uncomfortable subjects come up in children's play, representation, and conversation. These are all points of conflict. When points of conflict arise in the inquiry-based classroom, intrapersonal or interpersonal conflict disrupts engagement. Flow is interrupted. Teachers may be tempted to revert to old scripts and to the kind of power hierarchy that they learned long ago, or they see more traditional teachers practicing…scripts that make us lose sight of the collaborative, relational, joyful ways that drew us to inquiry-based education in the first place.

Teacher Scripts

Scripts are mechanisms that structure teachers' responses to conflict and challenges in a defined way. They take the most creative and autonomous tasks in teaching out of the teacher's hands. Remillard and Reinke (2012) describe the use of scripts in the classroom in this way.

> In this process, teachers are 'deskilled' or treated as conduits for the ideas of others. The label 'teacher-proof' is often used to characterize curriculum materials that attempt to override teacher authority and decision-making

in their design. In recent years, the term 'scripted curriculum' has been invoked to depict teachers' guides that tightly structure or direct teaching actions. In some cases, the guide literally takes the form of a script; in other cases, teacher actions are not fully scripted but the guide provides a narrowly prescribed path for instruction.

Scripts are calls for action without thinking. They are codified practices employed without much cognitive engagement or critical thinking on the part of the teacher. They tend to allow a teacher to abdicate responsibility for problem-solving and may not teach children what you truly intend. Think of a scenario in which a child runs up to the teacher complaining that another child took the toy he was playing with. Say the script leads the teacher to approach the "perpetrator," tell him off, and give the toy back to the complaining child. This practice squanders the teacher's opportunity to listen. It misses a chance to help the complainer express his feelings and desires, and it fails to support the perpetrator (if indeed he is so) to respond to the expression of the other. So much positive learning is left on the table when narrow expectations and expressions make up the bulk of classroom management!

A "narrowly prescribed path for instruction" is incompatible with teachers' creative problem-solving, autonomy, use of imagination, and possibly their deep engagement with teaching and learning. Curriculum teachers' manuals that tell you what to say and even what the children's response will/should be are full of scripts. Teachers may use scripts for classroom management, such as "123 eyes on me," or a flick of the lights to get children's attention. National and regional early childhood conferences are replete with workshops for the dissemination of scripts (how-to's), and teachers flock to them. YouTube videos and how-to Pinterest pages tout these scripts as necessary, and teachers often delight in finding a new script to address challenges in the classroom. They may collect these scripts and share them as "the best way to…."

Scripts may be labeled "tricks," "hacks," or "10 easy ways to…" They are suited to "shooting from the hip" and can often be characterized as reacting and not particularly responsive to the situation or to the child. Scripts have a way of allowing teachers to teach without having to engage creatively. Using them can inhibit the growth of the child and of the teacher. But teachers embrace them for the certainty and security they offer, and those things are comforting. They are often passed in whole cloth from teacher to teacher. And so, the life cycle of these scripts is eternal.

I have witnessed teachers who were committed to inquiry-based education stop and freeze in the face of a major sticking point. They had run out of ideas for what to do next. So, they responded to the sticking point in a way that hobbled the children's research. For example, they may have become uncomfortable with where a class conversation seemed to be going, and in trying to push the dialogue back to the original topic, the conversation lost its steam and never met its potential. Or, not knowing how to help a child get unstuck in drawing something, succumbed to the child's request to "draw it for me," thereby missing an opportunity to support skill development and confidence. The teacher may know a limited script will not have the results she wants. But she may not know how to address sticking points without resorting to instant fixes that limit or derail the very inquiry they are trying to support.

Now, we all use scripts of some sort. They represent shortcuts of a sort. For example, when I get ready to leave the house, I might prepare in a certain order...shoes, then a bag, then keys. It keeps me from forgetting something; if I were to head out without one of those items, I would recognize its absence. In a sense, the script allows me to operate without having to think. All well and good for the routine, relatively meaningless actions of daily life. But do we really want to be on automatic pilot with something as significant as being with the children in our care? We might ask ourselves, "Does this script keep me from truly engaging in something significant?" "Does it limit the possibilities available to the children and me?" "Does it hinder my growth or keep me from being intentional about what I do?" In the leaving-the-house scenario, the answer is most likely no. But in the classroom? There, examination of frequently used scripts is warranted.

I taught kindergarten in a K-12 independent school for eleven years through the 1980s. The school decided to add a Junior Kindergarten in 1990 for children who were eligible for kindergarten by chronological age but were deemed "not ready" for it (I knew then it would have been better to see the "problem" as an opportunity to change the kindergarten to meet the needs of the children, but that is not what happened). I had the opportunity to start the JK program without pre-determined curricular guidelines. It allowed me to look hard at the assumptions and scripts I had learned in my graduate education classes and from more experienced teachers at the beginning of my career. I was amazed to discover how many common school practices…such as using clothespins to manage how many children may play in each interest area …either worked against the children's best interests or were in place for the convenience of the teachers. Many of those practices lead to fewer learning opportunities for children. In that first JK year, I got to ask myself why we do what we have done, keep what seemed to be most respectful to the children and most conducive to the growth I wanted to see and toss what wasn't. Having a landscape free of old scripts for environment, time, and pedagogical choices allowed me to build a program intentionally, based on what I would one year later learn the educators in Reggio Emilia call my image of the child. Only those practices that satisfied my questions, "Why?" and "What's being learned here?", a phrase that I have heard Lilian Katz use, survived interrogation. That was the beginning of my work with flexible protocols as an antidote to teacher scripts.

Flexible Protocols as an Alternative to Scripts

How do we transition from scripts to thinking, from direction-following to research? Analyzing scripts for consistency with our values about teaching and learning can let us know which ones we must put aside in order to engage fully with children's research. I'll admit it can feel a bit like throwing oneself into the deep. The thinking teacher knows she should trust the process, trust the children, and trust herself. But she also knows she will encounter conflict in this work. Sticking points are inevitable in pedagogy that doesn't pretend to know all the answers in advance. Even with the intention to engage fully with children in their research, the teacher might be tempted to resort to old, unexamined scripts when points of conflict arise. But she values thoughtfulness too much to succumb to the certainty that scripts offer.

For a teacher to examine old scripts and toss what doesn't work in favor of participating in collaborative research with children, he needs to call on certain dispositions and strategies. He needs the disposition to listen, curiosity about what children's expressions really mean, and the expectation that the children in his life will present with daily moments of brilliance. He needs to embrace uncertainty, be ready to listen more than he talks, and be willing to try. But sometimes good intentions are not enough. A teacher may not feel safe eschewing old scripts if he doesn't have an alternative plan. Does he follow well-established and static scripts with a certain but limited outcome, or does he forge a new path with an eye toward practice that honors the competence of the children in front of him? He may appreciate guidelines that leave room for him to direct his imagination, creativity, and research. These guidelines…or protocols…are like pocketsful of resources, ready to frame an experience with children in the way most helpful to that teacher and those children at a particular point in time.

Flexible protocols can be there for this teacher in the face of common challenges like research projects getting stuck or not emerging at all. Or social conflict that threatens to disrupt play or collaboration. Or children getting stuck and frustrated trying to represent their ideas. They are guides that the thinking teacher can use to navigate the path of decision-making when he finds himself asking, "What do I do now?"

The protocols do not prescribe "say this" and cannot be characterized as tricks or hacks.

They are guides that leave room for thinking, responsiveness, and open-endedness.

Over the years, in response to myriad sticking points while working alongside children, I developed or borrowed and adapted many flexible protocols that have helped keep the teachers I have worked with and me in a zone where children remain central, and where old scripts are not needed. They have been a scaffold for me as a teacher to stand on when I didn't know what to do. And they have helped to keep the adults in the room consistent with each other with everything from sharing an image of the child, to our values around materials and how we value and use conflict.

I once had an assistant teacher who painted as a hobby. Following her interest, she negotiated with the three other teachers in the room so she could supervise the painting easels every day. I soon noticed that she struggled to embrace the values by which the rest of us were guided: representation is central to learning; children learn through creating story through painting (which could be one object, a scene, an idea, or a feeling); and there is value in reciprocity between graphic and verbal representation. We wanted her to ask the children about their paintings and encourage them to revisit their paintings if they thought of new ideas as they were articulating their meaning. We wanted to see the children's skills and confidence in representation grow. However, this teacher did not engage in dialogue with the children about their paintings. She gushed about every painting, calling it a masterpiece. In her response to children's work, she did not distinguish between exploring the medium and attempting to represent, and she did not support children if they got stuck or if they struggled to engage. We needed the vocabulary and support for dialogue among all the teachers about our role, which we found in the protocols for responding to children's representation (see Chapters 6 and 13).

In this kind of conflict…battling philosophies…having a flexible protocol around supporting children's representation can make the philosophy transparent. Without transparency, dialogue does not take place, and nothing changes. We may know that the children are getting conflicting messages but might not have a way to support teachers unfamiliar with the philosophy to move forward. Flexible protocols can serve as foundational agreements all the adults in the classroom use in adult-child interactions, in supporting research, and in using conflict for good.

Consider This

- When have you experienced Flow? What were you doing? Why do you suppose you experienced it then?
- What challenges to pedagogical flow affect the play and research the children in your class engage in?
- What scripts have you adopted in your teaching? Examine them. Which ones serve the children, and which do not? Which ones would you like to replace?

References

Csikszentmihalyi, M. (1990) *Flow: The Psychology of Optimal Experience*. Harper.

Makiguchi, T. (1930). *Complete Works of Tsunesaburo Makiguchi*, (in Japanese). Daisan Bunmeisha, Vol. 5, p. 124.

Remillard, J. & Reinke, L. (2012). "Complicating Scripted Curriculum: Can Scripts be Educative for Teachers?" University of Pennsylvania AERA 2012 Vancouver, British Columbia, Canada.

II
Flexible Protocols: Tools for the Back Pocket of the Thinking Teacher

A pedagogist or a pedagogical leader working with a teacher who has encountered a sticking point asks herself what that teacher needs to get unstuck. Can the teacher talk it through with a colleague and get unstuck that way? Or does he need a flexible protocol of some sort, a touchpoint, a mantra, or modeling? Rarely do teachers have the advantage of an in-the-moment pedagogical companion. But what if there were a guiding framework that supported the teacher who is asking himself the questions that inevitably come up in working with children and their research?

When I began to see myself as a teacher-researcher in the early 1990s, I found myself pretty much alone and with few resources at first. I read what little I could find published about the Reggio Emilia philosophy at the time, but I knew of no one in my area exploring Reggio principles in the classroom. Eventually, I found an online discussion group with others around the world who were asking the same questions I was asking, and I joined a consortium of educators from all over the US (The Lugano-Reggio Collaborative) who gathered periodically (including in Reggio Emilia) to grapple with questions like "What does Reggio inspiration look like in an American context?" and "What is the Italian educators' image of children's research?". But on a day-to-day basis it was up to me to do the research in answer to the myriad questions that kept bubbling up in my mind. These were questions as basic as "How do I set up the classroom environment to support the kind of learning I want to see?" and as complex as "What is the reciprocity between individual intelligence and group intelligence?" With constant reference to the thinking of educators in Reggio Emilia, I developed flexible protocols, which my teaching assistants and I tested and subjected to frequent reiteration over three decades. Until I retired from teaching, the protocols continued to evolve. Now I offer them to you, with the expectation that they will once again be subject to trial, examination, and reiteration. If you have wished for a resource that does not reduce to a superficial fix what you know is complex and, in many circumstances, unknowable ahead of time, I hope you will consider the possibilities of the protocols in this book.

You may already have developed your own set of open-ended protocols that honor the strength and agency of the children you work with and guide your decision-making in the face of sticking points. But if you haven't, or the ones you have developed don't lead to the resolution of sticking points to your satisfaction, I offer the following flexible protocols as guidelines that you can keep as referents, protocols through which you can funnel your imagination, creativity, and research to address sticking points. These protocols are resources that you can use in a way that is most helpful to you and to the children with whom you work. They are systems that you can use responsively. They are open frameworks for restoring pedagogical Flow. Some of the protocols offer structure and language to use with children in a way that does not usurp children's intent or "help" too much or too little. Some offer children support to tackle problems in cognitive and social challenges. All of the protocols are guidelines, not scripts…scaffolds, not "methods"… to address sticking points that interrupt pedagogical Flow.

6

The Environment and Small Systems

Small systems are mini-protocols the teacher-researcher can use as scaffolds for interaction in the classroom. They offer frameworks for children and teachers to navigate flexibly the situations that occur naturally when children have choice, voice, and interdependence in a classroom. Like the larger protocols, small systems can be an antidote to the temptation to rely on scripts to head off conflict.

Whether you are aware of it or not, you set up small systems in your classroom. Your environment sends a strong message about the expectations and values of the classroom. The way you talk to the children does, too. How materials are arranged lets children know if they are to be distributed by teachers or are accessible to them. How you approach problems, both social and cognitive, sends a strong message and models how you would like children to approach problem-solving. Since your small systems will be the children's teachers alongside human educators, it is best to be aware of them and set them up intentionally. To begin with, you might have a conversation with colleagues about what, exactly, you would like the children in your care to learn. Take a comprehensive view. Think about what will serve the children their whole lives, not just today and not just to prepare them for the next grade in school. What do you want for them (see Chapter 2)? What dispositions and habits of mind do you want to foster? From there, examine your existing small systems. Do they support collaboration and interdependence, or do they encourage children to "do their own work?" Do they turn children toward each other when there are problems, or do they send children to the adult in the room before they think about the problem? Does your language encourage children to recognize and own their intent and develop the disposition to follow their curiosity? Where is the teacher in the classroom? Is she central, or does she blend into the community of learners?

A Rich Environment

The classroom environment is more than a "small" system, in that it offers invitations for exploration and engagement, inspires wonder and curiosity, and supports relationships among children and between teachers and children. It presents the conditions for the learning that will happen in the space. It reflects the thinking and life of those who spend their time in it. I include in the term "environment" not only physical space but also the interactions within it and how time is organized. Among the characteristics of an environment conducive to children's research are:

- Materials in the classroom are ordered so children can access them as needed.
- The learning space is beautiful and provocative and invites relationships among children, between children and teachers, and with the environment itself.
- It is transformable by children and adults.
- It inspires wonder and supports deep engagement.
- It is responsive to the culture of the children and adults who teach and learn there.
- Children are able to exercise choice (of what to do, what materials to use, etc.) with systems in place to support work in progress.
- Time for deep engagement is planned for on a daily basis.

In many ways, a good classroom environment will turn children toward each other. Part of learning is being able to bounce one's theories and ideas off others, to try them out, and to see the responses they get. The classroom environment (considered in Reggio Emilia "the third teacher") can isolate children or invite them to collaborate. Step back and look at your space from a child's height. Does it call children together or have you created the equivalent of the individual work-mat? Are there spaces where only one child can work or are most opportunities open to small groups? Is the easel set up so painters can paint side by side and talk as they do, or do children paint in isolation? Is your expectation that children will build separate structures on the block platform, or do the setup and expectations invite collaboration? Are there tables where children can sit both beside and across from other children? Do you have paper big enough to accommodate multiple drawers/painters? Can children choose how they want to work: at a table, on the floor, etc., with many friends, a few, or alone? Do not underestimate the importance of the message the environment sends to children. If you watch carefully, you will see their response. Is it what you hoped it would be? If not, what changes can you make that will encourage what you want to see?

Children's deep engagement in what they are doing relies upon a rich environment. Without it, a teacher-researcher would have little to observe. I recall one kindergarten classroom I visited where every day started with the children completing tasks in a handwriting workbook. This was what the whole first hour of the day looked like every day. For this hour, the environment (including expectations) did not support the children showing the teacher who they were or what they were thinking. There was little for the teacher to observe or document except, perhaps, that several of the children simply could not engage with that workbook! When they had finished their assignment, the children could play with the few materials available: a few blocks in a basket, modeling clay, and paper. The children who simply could not engage with the workbooks wandered the classroom, talked to friends, or simply sat in front of their workbooks, silent. They never got to work with the materials, as limited and limiting as they were. One teacher sat reviewing the workbook pages with each child, and the other kept trying to get the uninterested children to sit down and work. The teachers had called me in because they were not seeing collaboration among the children. But it wasn't the lack of a disposition to collaborate that kept it from happening. I observed children trying to get collaborative endeavors going. But they were limited by the environment, specifically its materials, expectations, and time.

In contrast, imagine a classroom where, in the first hour of the day, some children are working on a collaborative block structure that summons imagination, storytelling, balance, and symmetry (the children's plan, not an assignment), some children choose to create stories with loose parts, some choose to paint using all the shades of blue they created the day before, and some are exploring the affordances (see Chapter 13) of folded cardstock. The teachers are traveling the classroom, observing, listening, documenting, helping the children who are making stories get them down on paper, and engaging in conversation with the children when appropriate. In this classroom, the problem is not that the children aren't able to show the teacher enough of themselves; it is that there may be too much to observe! Could the children in the first scenario have learned about letters and how they go together to make words in another, more constructive way? The teachers thought not, but I disagree.

See resources at the end of the book for inspiration as you think about the "third teacher" in your classroom.

Developing a Culture of Community

Teaching at a girls' school sometimes offered some interesting insights into the origins of social constructs. In particular, I noticed a phenomenon related to the children's drive for belonging: the advent of exclusion. When the girls were around five-and-a-half, they became able to classify by the attributes objects had and by the attributes they did not have. At about the same time, year after year, they started to create "clubs," to which some were invited and some were not. So conflict, both inner and external, arose. I hypothesized that the deeper intent behind forming these clubs was to understand the role of exclusion in belonging. Belonging was, of course, a desire (and a right) of all. I wondered if the children associated clubs with exclusion because their sense of belonging was not strong enough to stand without it. This was not what we wanted to see. I hypothesized that if we were to grow the children's sense of community, they might not be so eager to create belonging through exclusion. Could we head off some of the othering that we knew could be a pathway to the mean-girl syndrome we observed with many of the older students in the school? Enter small systems for the culture of community and belonging, designed to support a sense that everyone belonged and everyone bore responsibility to the group.

- Wherever possible we set up the environment so that every interest area could accommodate a group greater than two.
- Unlike every other classroom in the school, we had communal supplies. The children did not have individual sets of pens, scissors, and markers. Rather, everyone used the array of tools available, and everyone was responsible for caring for them.
- Rather than set up a system where children had to clean up their space when finished because we said so, we asked them to be sure the space was ready for the next friend who wanted to use it.
- Most children started the year building parallel to each other on our large block platform. We encouraged collaborative building in this way: inevitably, the platform got crowded, and the children complained. We welcomed that moment as the catalyst to a conversation in which we asked the children how they could work together with their two separate ideas to make one big structure. It was always a wonderful moment when we witnessed the children's delight at what collaboration could accomplish and how it felt.
- Eventually, the children would consider the massive block structure they had spent many days working on finished. Often the groups creating such structures had fluid membership. Imagine trying to ferret out who "made the mess" to create ownership and responsibility for cleanup! Good

thing we didn't want to do that. Instead, some of the builders would inform everyone at a class meeting that it was time to clear the block platform. Before the children made plans for the rest of the morning, everyone gathered at the block platform. We put on clean-up music, usually from "World Playground" (Putamayo, 1999) or some other upbeat collection, and everyone...children, teachers, and parent helpers...participated in the cleanup. When the massive job was complete, the children reveled in the empty-and-ready block platform, and they often did a celebratory and joyful dance on top of it. Of course, in the beginning, some children preferred not to participate in the cleanup effort. And some didn't know how to organize themselves in the face of such a large task. So, we adults were there to support them. "Can you find more blocks like this one?" we might ask. Or "Will you help me fold this big cloth?" In time, the joy was contagious, and collaborative cleanup spread to other big messes. We supported that evolution by inviting children who had finished tidying up their workspaces to help others who had more left to do.

Collaborative cleanup.

- Another small system aimed at building community was the identification of experts. When a child's shoe needed tying, and she couldn't do it herself, rather than dispatch the task ourselves, we might invite a good shoe-tyer to help. If someone was struggling to draw or write something, we might say, "You're having trouble drawing a star? I remember that Ella drew a star the other day. Would you like to ask her to tell you how she did it?" In this way, we were turning the children toward each other.
- We utilized another small system when a child told another that the image she had drawn or painted didn't look like it should. The critic may have been trying to be helpful (or not, but the power of criticism to injure is learned), and we wanted to use this tiny conflict for good. I have observed teachers chastise the critic, probably as a habituated script. Then the critic, who may have been trying to be helpful, would feel shame. And the artist wouldn't learn that she could have been more satisfied with a revision. Instead, when we heard children critique each other's work, we framed the interaction as positive. We invited the artist to ask the critic what the piece needed to look like the intended subject. This offered a more benign perspective for the artist (and for the critic if that wasn't what she intended!). Usually, once she had offered her insight, the critic was invested. And once the artist revised her piece, she was more satisfied with her work and usually received affirmation from the critic. In fact, one of the protocols we used when children declared themselves finished with a representation, especially if it was drawn/painted/sculpted from life, was to invite the child to check in with a friend to see if her piece was missing anything. This was particularly useful when we were trying to support the development of a reasonable satisfaction bar (see the subchapter on the Study Protocol, Chapter 13).

A child helps another with her clay sculpture.

♦ "Are You OK?" We used this small system as an alternative to asking children to apologize when they had offended or hurt another child and to help children know how to care for each other. We modeled and set an expectation that children would turn toward the child who is hurt (physically or emotionally), no matter what happened or by whose hand. The words we invited children to use were, "Are you OK?" This made the injured child feel seen and cared for. If that's all she needed, she would say yes, and play would usually continue. If she needed more, and she said, "No," we coached the child who was asking (and who well might be the cause of the injury) to ask, "What do you need?" or "How can I help?" She might ask if the injured party needed a glass of water (which she would get), some pats on the back, or something more related to the injury (a band-aid or another chance to try, for example). Almost always, being cared for by the person who hurts you (or a bystander if the injury was an accident) makes the wounded feel better. In addition, the child who has hurt another is doing something to make amends, repair the relationship, and get back into play. Everyone leaves the situation feeling better. No othering occurs. Everyone still belongs.

What were the results of the research project about clubs, belonging, and exclusion? After putting all the small systems in place, we observed that the children still created clubs when they were about five and a half, with one big change. Without our forbidding the clubs or the exclusion, or trying to manage them from the teacher's height, the children set out to get as many others as possible to join their clubs. We were amazed at the shift in priorities. Children still had special friends. But everyone had a sense of belonging to the entire group. The children didn't need exclusion to understand belonging. We kept those small systems going in subsequent years with the same results.

Occasionally, I get to reconnect with the parents of JK alumnae who are much older now, and they report that their children had made other school friends through the years, but they always kept a special sense of community with their JK classmates. I couldn't help but wonder what would have happened if this small system (or all of them?) had continued throughout their schooling. And what if those who joined the class in later years had similar experiences? If the JK alums carried forward a tiny piece of the understanding of belonging they constructed when they were five, past graduation from high school, what might the implications be for our divided society, where othering seems to reign?

Constructing Agreements

In classrooms with interest areas (blocks, dramatic play, making space, and so on), I've seen (and, before I knew better, used) teacher-assigned limits of how many children can be at an interest area using clothespins, charts, signup sheets, or numbers displayed at an area to indicate limits. I've observed teachers use scripts to manage how children will move from area to area, for example, management that limited choice and that set an amount of time a child may be at a certain area. I've witnessed teachers enforce a rule that materials stay in their assigned areas. Even in preschool classrooms, I've seen Class Rules posted, either composed by teachers or, perhaps worse, on a purchased poster. All these scripts limit possibilities and don't give children an opportunity to try collaborative regulation or become more aware of problems and possible solutions. They privilege management over the valuable practice of generating agreements. Of course, failing to do anything to support the arrangements for play could invite negative conflict and chaos. But what if we invited children's participation in creating social agreements and a framework for peaceful movement within the classroom? In doing so, we'd be supporting the growth of children's executive function and personal resources, such as a sense of competence and autonomy.

When we tell children, "These are the rules that you must follow," the directive is something we are doing *to* them. Obeying the rules requires children to exert impulse control without appreciation for why the rule is necessary (even if you've told them). Obeying the rules does not require empathy, a sense of fairness, or a deep sense of community and belonging. I have often heard children declare what is right based on rules they must follow but miss the connection between the rule and their own actions. This seems to be a developmental stage in the growth of impulse control. Working with children to generate agreements supports that development while making transparent the relationship between social agreements and a strong sense of community.

I never sat down with a group of children and declared we were now going to write agreements for our class. We negotiated our agreements more organically. When there was a problem, either a child or a teacher would broach the subject in a meeting, and we'd work together to come up with a solution and an agreement.

Collaborative agreements may be negotiated "on-demand" to address areas of tension in the classroom. I found them particularly useful when one group of children wanted to play in a way that worried other children. For example, if a small group is engaged in big, wild play with "bad guys" chasing other children, and the other children object, the teacher (or if they had had experience solving problems this way, the children) may call a meeting so that the worried children can articulate their point of view to the bad guys. We want the children to expect that they can negotiate until an agreement is made with which everyone is satisfied. The negotiation between Chasers and Chasees might look like this:

Chasee:	We don't like it when you chase us with angry voices. It scares us.
Chaser:	We like to chase!
Teacher:	A Chasee said it scares them when you chase them. Chasee, what would be better?
Chasee:	Don't ever chase.
Teacher to Chasers:	Is that OK with you?
Chasers all at once:	No!
Teacher:	Chasers still want to chase. We need an idea about how to chase *and* everybody feel safe. Chasers, do you have an idea?
Chaser:	Chase just a little.
Chasee:	No.
Teacher:	Chasee, you don't like Chaser's idea. What is your idea?
Chasee:	We could say STOP if we're scared.
Chasee:	What if they don't hear us?
Chaser:	You could do this with your hands *and* say STOP.
Teacher:	What will you do if someone says STOP and puts their hands out?
Chaser:	Go fast the other way.
Teacher:	What do you think, Chasees?

Chasees try saying STOP and putting out their hands. They seem satisfied and agree to try the system.

Teacher:	So, this is your agreement: Chasers can chase, but if someone says STOP and puts out their hands, the chasers will go fast the other way. Yes?

This is a simple example, but even with more complex issues, the teacher supports the children to articulate their points of view and listen to and respond to each other. She helps them follow this system: Child A suggests a solution to a problem. If Child B doesn't like that idea, it is their turn to suggest an idea, which does not have to be accepted by Child A, but if not, it's Child A's responsibility to come up with the next idea and so forth. Children come to understand…and value…the idea that they must stay with the negotiation until all agree and that everyone has a responsibility to participate in forming the agreement. They find and use their voices. They feel heard. They maintain their sense of agency. And they are invested in the agreement, so they are likely to hold each other responsible.

This is not to say that we never institute an adult-generated rule for safety's sake. But it behooves us to examine what really constitutes safety rather than convenience or habit. For example, rules to keep everyone safe when crossing a road or respecting the boundaries of a fence on the playground may not be subject to agreement. But does safety require total silence in an absolutely straight line before we leave the classroom? An unexamined rule risks missing an opportunity for larger learning (e.g., what is really important when you are leaving the classroom and entering a public space and why?).

Collaborative Management

Conflict can be a catalyst for collaborative agreements. I have observed that children are more likely to be accountable and hold each other accountable for agreements that they have constructed with their community than they are for rules given to them. I always welcomed opportunities to address management-related challenges with the children. For example, on the first day of school, we placed no limits on how many children could play in the dramatic play space. It was a popular choice, and at one point in the day, there were inevitably so many children in the space that play was not particularly satisfying for anyone. When this happened, I initiated a class conversation about the problems I observed in the play space, not saying there were too many people, but sharing my observation that the children were bumping into each other, or the props were on the floor, and no one could walk, or whatever I actually observed. The children usually joined in with their own complaints. I wondered aloud how they might solve the problem and invited the children to think with me. Typically, a few children thought they should limit the number, but other children suggested other systems (though, interestingly, never clothespins!). The group negotiated and came up with a plan, which I might have thought was possible but not likely to work. If so, I did not quash their agreement but suggested a trial period, after which they would revisit to assess how it was going.

In my experience, children's agreements often work, but not always. But by the time the group revisited the agreement about the dramatic play area, they were invested in the problem and its solution. When they saw that their first idea didn't work, they suggested another meeting to discuss other possibilities. Sometimes, no second agreement was necessary because after wrangling with the problem for a few days, the children understood the problem well enough that they didn't choose to play in the area if it looked full or they engaged in negotiation, asking, "Will you tell me when you're finished?" or "Can I be the mommy who goes away on a trip?" and joined the play in a creative way.

"They Won't Let Me Play"

Inner conflict can occur when a child wants to join ongoing play and either doesn't know how or is/feels at risk of rejection. My assistant teacher and I wanted to empower children to ask to play and respond to those asking to play. So, we set up a system to support the flow of children into ongoing play. We honored children's wishes if they wanted to play alone (it was rare). But when there was a group playing, and someone wanted to join, we were uncomfortable allowing the group to reject her and wield power through exclusion. We valued relationship and community and wanted to foster a sense of belonging for all the children. Exclusion just didn't feel good for anyone except the excluders, and they deserved to experience a sense of belonging without having to exclude anyone. We knew that relationships are the antidote to othering. So we set an expectation, which we expressed as, "If they want to play, you find a way," much like Vivian Paley's "You can't say you can't play" (Paley, 1992). In some years, we were able to "find" this idea with the children through creating an agreement. In others, the opportunity to solve the problems created by exclusion collaboratively did not present itself before we needed the rule, and we adults introduced the idea.

The system was this: You ask to play. When the group says yes, you ask what's happening and what part you can play. You can agree, you can negotiate a different role, or you can decline. But you can't go in, take over, and change the play, at least not directly. The children learned that they had the power to influence how play went once they were engaged in it, through negotiation. They just couldn't come in and destroy what was ongoing. To some degree, this approach headed off the tendency of some to deny access to the approaching child for power's sake. To the group already playing, we said, "If they want to play, you find a way." We didn't leave the children to it. If a child sought our help, perhaps saying, "They won't let me play," we asked if she wanted to ask to join the play. Often, especially early in the school year, the response was, "I did ask! They said no." Then, we asked if the child wanted us to go with her when she asked again to play. We were there to support the approaching child as she did so. The group usually borrowed from the adult presence and agreed. Then we supported the new member of the group to inquire about what was happening in the play and what part she could play. We were there to support the group in welcoming the new player. And we were there if negotiations about roles were happening, using a special protocol (The ACIC Protocol, Chapter 7) to support the children to do as much of the negotiation as they could. In time, they were competent and confident at entering and welcoming others into play. Once the children adopted this small system, we teachers were called to offer support rarely and usually only when situations were more complex than usual.

The Planning Protocol

One of the "hopes" we hold for children, articulated in Chapter 2, is that they develop "awake minds": awareness of where they are and what they are doing, an ability to plan and follow through, and a consciousness that develops with maturity out of the intuitive state of the toddler, all elements of executive function. Because we wanted to set the environment and expectations so that children could experience making decisions, we arranged for long periods of self-directed engagement, usually in small child-created groups. Children could choose to play, construct, represent, and engage in research during these times, requiring them to make decisions about what to do. Early in the year, many children seemed to make decisions about where to go and what to do intuitively. They wandered the classroom and "landed" somewhere without having planned to do so. They appeared to leave play and those with whom they were playing without consciously making a decision to do so; they acted and then found themselves where their bodies had taken them. The research question, "How can we support children's awakening minds?" led to the development of a small system we called the Planning Protocol. Quite simply, the protocol involves asking children, "What is your plan?"

Articulating a plan nudges the transition from one endeavor to the next into a more cognitive realm, where language regulates action. Once in that state, the child can make other decisions: what he wants to do, with whom to play, what materials he needs, and what steps he may need to take to realize his intent. Were he still in his intuitive state, he would not be making those choices consciously.

We used the Planning Protocol in a number of contexts. Here's how the protocol might look at the beginning of the day. A child arrives at school in the morning. He unpacks and greets his friends and teachers, and he may declare a plan ("I'm going back to the house I was making yesterday.") If he doesn't articulate a plan, the teacher prompts him, "What is your plan?" He will know what the possibilities are because, for the most part, the environment, rich with opportunities, is familiar to him. Perhaps the teacher's question reminds him that he wants to go back to a place where he engaged in particularly satisfying play the day before. Perhaps he has work in progress. Perhaps he remembers that he didn't get to do something he wanted to the day before (opportunity cost!), and he'd like to do it today. Declaring a plan can help children with the transition that starting a new day represents. Some children prefer to look around a bit first. You'll want to honor a child's need to acclimate before making a plan, recognize when acclimating turns into wandering aimlessly, and inquire about the child's plan somewhere in between.

Asking "What is your plan?" communicates an expectation that the child has an idea about what he wants to do. The youngest children or early language learners may just point to the block platform, and the teacher can clarify: "You want to build something with blocks?" If he doesn't know what he wants to do, the teacher may walk around with him a bit to help him remember what the possibilities are. Once he makes a choice, she might help him verbalize: "I want to play with blocks." As children's language grows, so does the articulation of their plan. At first, they may indicate generally where they want to go. Soon, their plans will become more specific; they will articulate what they plan to make or explore and with whom.

If your morning meeting is followed by self-directed play, representation, or project work, you might also invite children to declare plans at the end of the meeting. This allows children to hear the plans of others, which can remind them of the possibilities and inspire new ideas. It also gives children a chance to solicit collaborators for a new or continuing endeavor.

You can also ask children to declare a new plan when they are leaving an interest area. I found that the transition from one interest area to another could be a point of inner conflict for some children. They may have finished what they were doing in the first area but need a little support to decide where to go next. They may start to wander away, but when asked about their next plan, they would seem to wake up and realize that they didn't really want to leave after all. I found that after answering the question, "What is your plan?" the children were able to transition to whatever was next with greater intention and purpose. When I felt they no longer needed a prompt to make the transition consciously, it was important that I bow out. With the help of this one question, we are looking to place control of the children's comings and goings not in the teachers' hands through management but in the children's hands as soon as they can take it on.

In my experience, before long the children became proficient at declaring a plan, using strategies to remember work in progress, and following through on a plan. They were able to transition from one interest area to another with intention and without teacher support.

Schedules for Deep Engagement

If our hope is that children will engage with ideas for longer and longer periods of time, our classroom systems will have to support that. We want to create a schedule as free from frequent interruptions as possible. A fragmented schedule creates superficial engagement. Children get used to and internalize the short time span and, anticipating interruption, may have difficulty getting into Flow. Opportunity cost can also affect engagement: if children know they have a short time to work and they want to do multiple things during that time, it is hard for them to become engaged in any of them. Whenever I could, I tried to prioritize long periods of self-directed play and/or work in research groups. Of course, we had appointments during the day: P.E. and lunch, for example. So, I scheduled class meetings and time in the outdoor classroom around a long "Projects and Play" period. This allowed us to have an hour and a half of uninterrupted time every morning and a slightly shorter time in the afternoon in which children could become deeply engaged in whatever they were doing. At the beginning of the year, as they were learning the new environment, children often spent only a few minutes at each interest area. However, the unhurried schedule and consistency of materials (once we introduced a medium, we only took it out of the environment when we were sure the children were no longer interested in it) allowed the children to stay absorbed in their work for longer and longer periods.

Work in Progress

The downside of deep engagement is that children can be loath to stop working when it is time to move on. As a point of conflict, this is the flip side of a desirable state, and it is manageable with a small system, "Work in Progress." It can be hard to stop working on something pleasurable, especially if you have to "destroy" your work by putting it away. The Work in Progress system gives children a tangible way to declare their intention to come back to their work. It is assurance that they can return and that the adults will help them remember. It is an invitation to the child to think flexibly, knowing that her work will be waiting for her at her next opportunity.

To make space for work in progress, you can arrange the environment intentionally, creating spaces for unfinished work so that it can be available to the children again later. For example, we had a dedicated block platform instead of asking the meeting space to double as a block area, where the children would have to put away their structures after play. We had shelves and special containers where the children could store more portable three-dimensional work in progress. Each child had a work-in-progress folder for two-dimensional small work. If the work in progress were a painting, the painter left her work on the easel, which was a message to other children that the painter was coming back.

Just giving the work children considered unfinished a name seemed to help them understand that they could continue it later. Knowing this, they were more willing to put their work on pause. Each child had a work-in-progress card that had their name and picture on it. When it was time to go to one appointment or another, we invited those who wanted to go back to their work later to leave their work-in-progress cards with their work (if we were going out of the classroom) or bring it to Meeting if that's where we were going. The cards were a tangible promise: you can return. As a result, children tended to muster greater

This child has returned to her work-in-progress after an interruption.

emotional flexibility when asked to stop working and change gears. When the children made plans at the end of Meeting, the cards were a reminder of their intention to return to their work. If we'd been out of the classroom, the children might have forgotten their work-in-progress plans by the time we returned. The cards were a reminder to the teacher, who could, in turn, remind the children of their plans. The cards had other uses as well. We kept them all together in a jar. When children were learning to write their names, the cards were useful as referents. When children wanted to write their friends' names, they were able to find the appropriate card either by the first letter of the name or by the photograph.

Consider This

- What small systems do you have in your classroom? Investigate them with a colleague. Do they match your values? Do you like what they yield?
- How does your environment "teach?"

♦ How does management in your classroom work? What do children learn from it? Does it privilege obedience or a sense of agency? Do the children learn to negotiate the environment on their own in time?

References

Paley, V. G. (1992). *You Can't Say You Can't Play*. Harvard University Press.
World Playground: A Musical Adventure for Kids. (1999) Putumayo World Music.

7

Flow Challenge

Social Conflict

Social conflict in the classroom disrupts play and work and, if unaddressed, can challenge children's sense that school is a safe place. Old scripts would tell a teacher to solve the children's problems so peace can return. Often, those scripts have the potential to leave children feeling confused and/or shamed, do not aim to repair wounded relationships, and afterward, children tend not to re-enter play at their previous level of engagement. They may abandon the play and do something else; or they may stay, and instead of collaborating, play parallel to each other. Conflict has created a full stop in the children's interaction, at least temporarily. Social conflict can be a huge sticking point in Flow for children and adults.

Consider the emotional fallout from social conflict. Play is disrupted, not only for the children involved in the conflict but possibly for all in the vicinity. Emotions run high, too high for much thinking to happen. Relationships may be damaged. If the teacher chooses the "Tell him you're sorry" script, children may experience anger, shame, or embarrassment. If the teacher chooses to solve the children's problems for them, the children learn much about power in the classroom. Who has it, who doesn't, who can be bullied, and who can be manipulated?

In many classrooms, the adults seem to own children's conflict. Even teachers who listen sometimes make judgments about who is right and who is wrong so quickly! What is being learned if the teacher solves the problem? Most likely not what we intend. Often, the child who offends another learns only that the teacher is more powerful than she is, and she has to comply. Equally important is what the offending child is not learning. She is not learning how to negotiate, how to consider the perspective of the other, how to use language to make her position known, and how to respond to the language of someone with a different perspective. Perhaps even more important is what the offended party is not learning: that she has a voice and can muster the courage to use it. Neither child is learning how to maintain or repair her relationship with the other (e.g., listen to the other and respond with kindness). What will happen the next time there is conflict? Have the children come away from the first experience more capable of solving problems? Or will the teacher's role as problem-solver for the children persist?

Social conflict in the classroom *can* be an opportunity. It can be the path toward two goals: One, that children use language to make their thoughts, feelings, needs, and ideas known. And two, that children respond positively to the language of others. Having a way to address social conflict while maintaining everyone's dignity and sense of safety and well-being serves children in a way that realizes everyone's ultimate intent: to belong. Having a protocol to help children acquire the skill and self-control to manage social conflict serves the teacher's goal: to move away from being "police of the classroom" and to create a state of harmony in the classroom.

A discussion with colleagues to address the question, "What do we want for the children when they face social conflict?" is a good first step in moving away from reliance on old scripts. Perhaps you will decide together that you would like children to become increasingly interdependent and less reliant on teacher support in the face of social conflict. You might want children to learn to negotiate with each other when there is conflict around ideas or actions. And, if there is conflict and play is disrupted, that children will be able to return to their earlier engagement once the problem is solved to their satisfaction. You might agree to privilege practices that encourage children to know and value the perspectives of others while developing their own voice and using it. Perhaps you and your colleagues will prioritize systems that help children develop the disposition and the skill to repair relationships when they are damaged by conflict.

The following story, in two parts, illustrates how a teacher might create the conditions for that learning.

> Five-year-old J'Quan is playing with a racecar in his kindergarten classroom. He puts the car down to attend to another part of his block-corner racetrack. Anthony, a newcomer to the block corner this morning, sees the racecar on the floor and picks it up. J'Quan, seeing that he is about to lose his car, quickly grabs it. A tug of war ensues, with both children angry and shouting; play is disrupted around the room, and a crowd of children gathers. The teacher arrives at the block corner to find both boys in tears.

Here is where some teachers might swoop in and make a decision *for* the boys: J'Quan had it first, so he should have it. Or J'Quan took it out of Anthony's hand, so Anthony should have it. Or she might even punish both boys for their emotional outbursts. Sound familiar? If we follow through with that trajectory, we will see that it results in shame, anger, or passivity...none of it conducive to learning or supportive of the boys' relationship.

Fortunately, J'Quan and Anthony's teacher understands that the boys can resolve this problem (and similar ones) in a way that will result not in anger or shame, but in growth of the boys' arsenal of strategies for resolving conflict, resulting in a stronger friendship between them. The teacher turns to the Adult-Child Interaction Continuum (ACIC).

The Adult-Child Interaction Continuum

The ACIC is a continuum of responses you can use when interacting with children who are facing a problem of one kind or another (not necessarily social conflict, but it is very helpful in that context). Social conflict can become emotion-laden quickly. The ACIC helps keep social conflict cognitive so that children can learn the language of negotiation. It also keeps the adult's emotions out of negotiations between children, holding the interaction in the cognitive realm. And it can help all the adults in the room be consistent when social conflict arises.

The continuum can be attributed, originally, to Dr. Charles Wolfgang, who mined various philosophies of adult-child interaction current at the time (personal communication, 1985). He created a continuum that ranged from essentially no intervention by the adult to physical intervention. Wolfgang's intention was that teachers would engage in some metacognition and find their comfort zones on the continuum. But I saw another possibility for the continuum, and he gave me permission to develop it. Using the same range of adult-child interactions, I framed it as a flexible protocol teachers could use to support children's social competence, confidence, and autonomy. It is a way in which teachers can know what support children need in the moment and a way for them to offer that support without doing more for the children than necessary. It is a way to help children learn to find their way into play, a way for them to find their voice in a social context, and a way for them to play without permanent disruption from social conflict. It is a way that relationships can be maintained and, if necessary, repaired, in the face of conflict.

The left side of the continuum represents minimum support from the teacher. The teacher doesn't need to help much, and just her presence gives children the support they need to engage in negotiation on their own. The right side of the continuum represents the maximum support from the teacher. The teacher engages in this level of intervention if the children can exercise little or no control over a situation, even when borrowing control from the teacher. Each increment going from left to right on the continuum represents a little more participation from the teacher to supplement the children's knowledge or control.

The aim of using the ACIC is that children will articulate their points of view to each other and respond to those of others in a way that will allow play and collaborative work to resume and, if necessary, the relationships to be repaired. In social conflict,

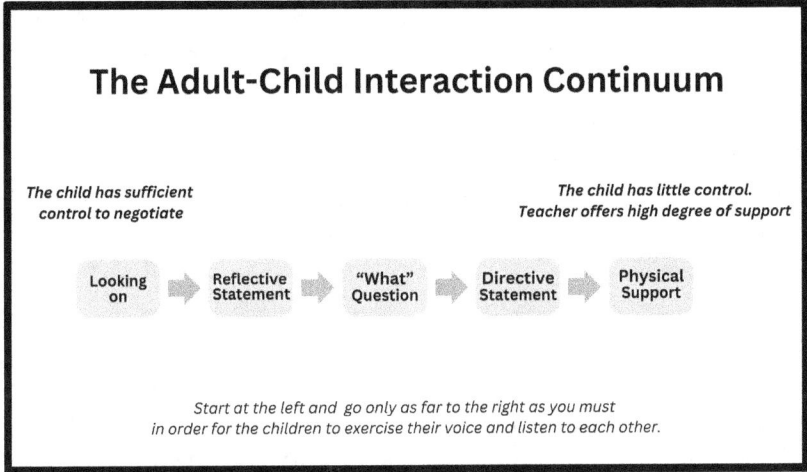

there may be an antagonist and an injured party…a child who has taken and a child from whom something has been taken, for example. The teacher will focus on the injured party first…the child who has experienced some sort of harm. This is because the injured child must first articulate his feelings, needs, desires, side of the story, etc., before negotiation can begin. We want this process to stay in the cognitive dimension, where learning happens. So, the teacher is careful to remain calm throughout the process.

The ACIC invites the full participation of all in the negotiation process. The teacher's role is to support the children emotionally and offer language and tools responsively as the children need them, until both parties are satisfied, at least to some degree.

Using the Protocol

Looking On
The teacher notices that tensions are arising in one part of the classroom. She approaches and observes (Looking On) so that she can ascertain what's going on and lend the emotional support of an adult's presence. Sometimes, if children know what to do but haven't thought of it yet or need emotional support to act, the

teacher's presence will be enough. Feeling supported, the child may say, for example, "Hey, I had that first. Please give it back." An adult's silent presence can be powerful for children; it is not to be underestimated. Children borrow from us all the time. They borrow from our emotional state: our calm, our blame, our distress, our confidence, and so on. Here is the story of an experience that brought to light, for me, the power of adult presence for children.

> One year the children in my class found interaction with each other particularly challenging. The first weeks of school were rife with arguments and affronts. The ACIC was in heavy play that Fall. As the children began to trust that they would be heard and as they began to use language more than bodies to communicate displeasure, they became more inclined to engage in collaborative work. One day I experienced the power of 'just my presence' in the children's ability to sustain play without disruption. A small group was working well at the block platform, constructing collaboratively. I was sitting at a distance, observing and documenting, ready to lend support if the children needed it. But because they had the language and, I thought, the emotional control to proceed interdependently, all was peaceful and constructive for quite a while. I was not aware that the children were borrowing heavily from my silent presence to maintain control. I was called away briefly, and within a minute, the entire scene fell apart. Agreements were broken, feelings were hurt, and tempers flared. The play was disrupted, and the children left the area. It was an ah-hah moment for me. The second I left, harmony left, too. It was an opportunity to experience just how powerful a silent adult's presence can be.

Timeliness is important at the Looking On stage of the continuum. If you wait too long to approach impending conflict, emotions may flare. Once that happens, the children can't think. All you can do to help is address children's emotions. They come away from the experience with no greater resources than they had before the conflict occurred. The ACIC aims to help children learn strategies for addressing social conflict in a way that satisfies everyone at least to some degree and does not interrupt play or work permanently. So, when you feel tension rising somewhere in the classroom, it is best to quietly approach as quickly as you can. You need not say or do anything at this stage; your presence may be enough.

Reflective Statement

If the teacher approaches and the child who has been injured does not articulate his position spontaneously, she moves one space to the right on the continuum and makes a reflective/nondirective statement. She articulates what she perceives is going on, addressing the injured party. "You look upset, J'Quan." Or "Anthony took your racecar?" That may be enough for J'Quan to say, "Hey, I had that first. Please give it back." The teacher pauses to see if J'Quan has both the language and the emotional fortitude to use it in this moment. If J'Quan does articulate his position, he has done what he needs to do, and the teacher turns her attention to Anthony. If not, she moves one step to the right on the continuum, addressing a What question to J'Quan.

What Question

The question is never "Why did you…?" Rather, it is the teacher trying to learn whether the child has the language to articulate his needs. She may ask, "J'Quan, what can you do to get your racecar back?" If J'Quan realizes that he does have a strategy he might say, "Ask for it back?" If he sounds unsure, the teacher will know that it is emotional support J'Quan needs, not language. She might say, "Yes. Can you ask for it back?" If J'Quan does not know what to say, the teacher knows a Directive Statement is probably warranted.

Directive Statement

Having learned that the child does not actually know what to say, the teacher tells the child what he can say to Anthony to get his truck back. The words she uses will depend on the language development or age of the child. She wants the child to be able to use the strategy on his own, so if a very young child is ready to use one or two words, perhaps the teacher says, "Tell Anthony," "Mine," or "Want it." With older preschoolers, the words she suggests the child say can be more sophisticated. "Tell Anthony, 'I was playing with it, and I would like it back.'"

While focused on the injured party, we never get to the Physical Intervention stage at the far right of the continuum. If the injured party cannot talk to the other child even when given the words and emotional support, then the teacher says something like, "It looks as if you aren't ready to ask for the racecar back. Let me help you find/make another one to play with." You might be thinking, "That's not fair!" But if you were to ignore the fact that the injured party can't ask for the item back, what would the children have learned? The injured party would have learned that he doesn't have to use words to get his toy back if the teacher will do it for him. He doesn't experience the power of language or develop confidence in interactions with peers. The antagonist would have learned (though he probably already knows) only that the teacher is bigger and more powerful than he is, but his friend has no power.

If, at *any* point on the continuum the injured party does ask for the toy back, and the antagonist gives it back, the teacher waits to see if the children return to their play. If they do, she can walk away. But if the injured party asks for the toy back and the other child does not give it back, the teacher returns to the left side of the continuum, this time focused on the antagonist. Of course, she's already present, so she doesn't need to approach. But she does wait a beat to see if the child responds to his friend's request. If he does not, she will make a reflective statement: "J'Quan asked for the racecar back." And she waits. Anthony may need to think about this for a beat. If he does not give the racecar back or articulate his case in a way in which J'Quan can participate, the teacher progresses to the What Statement.

What Statement
"J'Quan asked for the racecar back. What can you do so you can both be happy?" If Anthony does not give the racecar back, we

don't know if he doesn't know what to do or if he is deciding not to. Regardless, the teacher moves to a Directive Statement if Anthony does not act for several seconds.

Directive Statement
"J'Quan asked for the racecar back. Please give it back." Now we know he knows what he should do. If he doesn't give it back, the teacher moves to Physical Intervention.

Physical Intervention
If Anthony still cannot give the racecar back or engage in negotiation, the teacher will repeat the directive statement, while gently, physically helping him give the racecar back. The teacher does not leave Anthony high and dry. She says, "Let me help you find/make another racecar," in hopes that the boys can resume play.

When the injured party has articulated his position and the antagonist has responded appropriately, the teacher quietly leaves the interaction and the children to their play. For the entire process, she has kept in mind the ultimate goal…the children's competence and confidence in negotiating through social conflict…and she has been careful not to let her emotion or agenda eclipse it.

As children acquire the tools for addressing social conflict, they are likely to initiate negotiation. The ACIC is as useful for supporting complex negotiation as it is for more simple scenarios like the J'Quan's and Anthony's. When children are engaged in negotiation and they are not frustrated or in a stalemate, you can try observing without intervening. In doing so, you are offering emotional support for their process while allowing them to use the resources they have to work things out. The teacher intervenes only responsively and not automatically, with as much support as the children need and not more.

Social and cognitive conflict may result in "yes-no-yes-no" interactions. So, you might want to set up some parameters for negotiation. The one I use is: if I have an idea but you reject it, then it is your responsibility to come up with another idea. If I agree, play can continue. If I don't, it is my turn to come up with an idea. And so forth. I have found that at first children tend to reject each other's ideas, sometimes on principle, but as they realize that they both get to be at least a little satisfied and that the more powerful or emotional child would not automatically "win," they begin to be more thoughtful about the negotiation. I am always a bit amused when, more times than not, after much back-and-forthing, the children settle on the first idea proposed. Once they are in agreement, play often resumes. My role in these negotiations is to be present and ready to support the children to use the protocol.

As with many of the flexible protocols in this book, I have found that when teachers use the ACIC protocol consistently, children begin to see its value and begin to use it on their own without requiring the teacher's presence. Until, that is, their disagreements become more complex and sophisticated. In those situations, there may be no antagonist or injured party. If children are tangling with issues of fairness, competing ideas or needs, or other more complex problems, they will still require a teacher's support through the ACIC, just on a different level. Because this is a *flexible* protocol, a teacher can adjust the protocol for social conflict at any level.

Just as flexibility of thinking comes into play during negotiation for the children, the supporting teacher, too, must muster flexibility. If she has in mind a particular outcome, but the children come up with and agree on something entirely different, she will need to go with the flow. If both parties are satisfied, the teacher must let go of her agenda and join the children in theirs. This is true not only in the face of social conflict but also during negotiations in children's research.

The Rest of the Story

When Anthony picks up the car and J'Quan objects, their teacher, sensing tension in that corner of the room, walks up to the boys, close enough to touch them (Looking On). Feeling slightly safer, J'Quan relaxes a bit, although Anthony still holds onto the car. The teacher says calmly, 'J'Quan, you were playing with the car and put it down to check on the other parts of your racetrack?' (Nondirective Statement) J'Quan nods but doesn't say anything to Anthony. The teacher wants J'Quan to understand that his words are what will get his car back. Kneeling at eye level and as close to Anthony as she is to J'Quan, the teacher pauses a moment and then says, 'What can you say to Anthony to get your car back?' (What Question) J'Quan looks at the teacher and says, 'I was playing with it first?' The teacher nods and smiles and, after a few seconds, says, 'And what do you want to ask Anthony to do?' J'Quan answers tentatively, 'Give me the car back?' Again, the teacher nods. She now knows that J'Quan has the language he needs but could use her emotional support to ask for the car back. J'Quan turns to Anthony and says, 'I was playing with it first. Can I have it back now?' Anthony gives the racecar back. J'Quan says, 'Here, you can have this truck. Wanna help me make the rest of the road?' The teacher, seeing that the boys have solved the problem and have resumed play, quietly leaves them to it.

Using the ACIC supports not only problem-solving but also the interdependence we hope children will develop within their learning communities: children supporting each other in play, and, when relationship and ownership are in conflict with each other, the former nudging the latter aside in importance.

Note: There's a safety clause in the ACIC. If you are worried that someone is about to be hurt physically, you would not begin with "Looking On." Rather, you'd pop to the right side of the continuum immediately to make sure everyone stays safe. Once any danger is averted, the teacher can begin with the Reflective Statement part of the continuum. If a child is emotionally flooded, the continuum will not be useful. Instead, the teacher will want to help the child regulate his emotions without adding to them with her emotions or trying to "talk it out." In that case, the teacher can consider the event information for the future so that she can offer the support of the ACIC sooner for that child and his friends.

I always shared the ACIC with parents during our first parent-teacher conferences of the year so that they would know how we were supporting children's social and emotional growth. Many parents reported later that they had adopted the protocol in their family interactions, and sometimes, a parent would confess that they'd tried it with a spouse!

Isn't the ACIC an Elaborate Script?

I suppose it could be used as one. But that is not the intention. The adult uses the continuum to determine what cognitive and emotional support children need in the face of conflict. In a sense, it is a research tool. It is meant to be used responsively. For example, a two- or three-year-old child may not have the language and/or the emotional control to respond to the teacher simply walking up to the site of conflict. The teacher knows the children, and she may choose to start at the reflective statement step, saying to a child who looks upset, "You didn't like it when your friend hit you." Realizing that the language the toddler uses must be simple, the teacher might say, "Tell your friend STOP!" When the toddler says STOP, the teacher would then address the child who hit and say, "Your friend looks sad when you hit her. Say, 'Are you OK?'" This is far more directive than you would be with an older preschooler. The language available to the offended party will be more complex, and the process of using the ACIC may help an older child self-regulate, where a toddler will need more co-regulation from the adult. The protocol will help you know the children and what they need from you at this moment. And then it will be important to allow for growth. Moving from left to right on the continuum each time there is conflict lets you recognize when the child who previously needed support all the way to the directive statement stage now only needs a non-directive statement in order to engage in negotiations.

Contrast the ACIC with the script, "Tell him you're sorry." The script leaves the interaction short, with the damaged relationship unrepaired. It leaves the injured party satisfied that he got what he wanted but also a little bit helpless, since he leaves the interaction with no greater strategy for having his needs and wants met than invoking the teacher's power. And it leaves the antagonist equally helpless or angry because he has given up the toy, and he may feel ashamed. Helplessness, anger, and shame all preclude learning what we would like the child to learn: that he is obligated to listen to the language of others and that he will always get an opportunity to repair what he has (maybe not intentionally) damaged.

Consider This

- ◆ What scripts have you used in the face of social conflict in your classroom? Do you feel differently about them now?
- ◆ Have you owned children's conflict instead of inviting them to negotiate until they are satisfied? How do you think the children felt afterward? How did you feel? Do you feel differently now?

8

Conversations for the Co-Construction of Theory

The Power of Conversation

Conversations for the co-construction of theory are a powerful element of children's research.

From the beginning of their lives, children construct theories ceaselessly about how the world works. Infants do this work by gathering information from their senses and acting on that information with their bodies. For the first years, as verbal language develops, children's expressions and explorations (i.e., their research) remain tied to action (gestures, exploration of materials and media, experimentation, etc.). Once they've reached a certain proficiency with verbal language, a new dynamic becomes possible: conversations for the co-construction of theory, in which children think together about a topic. Whether they come to a consensus in these conversations is immaterial. The very act of engaging in dialogue is enriching to the individual and the group. These conversations for the co-construction of theory about how the world works become a new medium of sorts, temporal and reliant on collaboration. Suddenly, there is a new way of knowing and a new avenue for developing group intelligence. The possibilities for children's collaborative research expand. Through these conversations, children learn to find and use their voices. They are exposed to the perspective of others and have an

DOI: 10.4324/9781003625568-11

opportunity to bounce the theories of others off their own experience and theories. They learn to think together. Conversations, both informal and during class meetings, can be instrumental in the development of the culture of a group.

We can take advantage of the diversity of perspectives that conversations uncover naturally. One of the gifts afforded us when having good conversations is that children hear and consider a variety of points of view. Those points of view may differ due to culture, family, community, and/or the individual. As witnesses to children's meaningful conversations and collaboration, we have the opportunity to support their embrace of the unfamiliar and consideration of differing viewpoints. We have the privilege of helping them experience a sense of belonging that transcends sameness. Of course, there are many ways teachers can honor the diversity in their classrooms. Facilitated conversations, in which thinking teachers support children to find and use their voices and consider the perspectives of others, are especially good opportunities to do so.

Co-Constructing Theory

> When we read unedited transcripts of children's conversations, we are often stunned by the complexity of their minds, their nuanced understanding of custom, human nature, and ... the dynamics of being friends. In particular, we are stunned by the logic they use to fill in the inevitable gaps in what they remember from direct experience.
>
> *George Forman (2014)*

As philosophers and scientists, children engage in research, unbidden. They construct theory about how the world works, whether we encourage it or not. We can support children's natural inclination toward intellectual growth by inviting them to tackle compelling ideas together, including through dialogue. When cognitive conflict arises in conversation, and as children articulate their theories and opinions, they engage in cognitive negotiation. And that can lead to significant and most satisfying growth in understanding, as well as in the disposition and ability to engage in conversation for the co-construction of theory. What might this look like?

Here is an excerpt from a blog post I wrote on a day when the children were surprised by rainbows on the walls of the classroom. All the children were five years old or nearly.

> This morning, the children were excited to see a 'rainbow' on the wall. Gigi posed a theory about where it came from, so when we went to Meeting I invited her to share her theory with everyone.
>
> In the ensuing conversation, the children posed multiple theories, ranging from what they'd heard from adults to their own (magical) theories. They reached no coherent consensus during the conversation. It was after the meeting, as they set out to test their theories, that a more coherent theory emerged.

Gigi:	The light moves. The light moves outside. It happened outside on the rocks.
Teacher:	How did the rainbow get in here?
Gigi:	It shines through the door. And then it forms something, and then it kind of turns into a rainbow.
Teacher:	Where does it turn into a rainbow? Outside or inside?
Livvy:	Outside!!!!
Gigi:	Outside.
Essie:	No, inside. It turns into a rainbow INSIDE.
Teacher:	Essie, where do you think it comes from?
Essie:	The walls. It bounces off the walls and catches light!
Teacher:	What bounces off the walls?
Claire:	The rainbow, she's talking about!
Elizabeth:	When I look at the light, a rainbow looks into my eyes.

Teacher:	What does that tell you?
Elizabeth:	The sun makes a rainbow.
Teacher:	How does it get on our wall?
Livvy:	I know! I think the air makes it float to the wall.
Livvy:	I know how you make a rainbow. You have to get a light. And then get a fishbowl, and then a rainbow comes.
Teacher:	That's how you make it? But do we have a fishbowl here? No? So there must be another way, too, huh?
Janelle:	Well, when rainbows go in your eyes, that means special things are gonna happen.
Minnie:	The rainbow moved!
Teacher:	The rainbow moved again?! How is it moving?
Hallie:	The wind!
Olivia:	'Cause it floats away to a different spot.
Claire:	I'm gonna keep my eye on that rainbow.
Holly:	I saw a rainbow before, and it came from outside, and it comes from the rain and the sun, and it has to be in the darkness to make it, so that's how it happened.
Teacher:	So do you think that rainbow was made when it was dark?
Holly:	Yeah, when it was night.
Gigi:	When we see rainbows at my Gram's, it's usually when we are in front of it, the rainbow is blocked.
Teacher:	What does it mean, blocked?
Gigi:	You can't see part of it.

I tried to block the rainbow with my hand.

Gigi:	See how it goes away?
Teacher:	Did it go away? Where is it now?
Gigi:	On your hand.
Child:	It's almost gone!
Teacher:	It is almost gone. Where will it go when it's gone?
Olivia:	Outside.

Livvy:	I think the rainbow fairy came last night. She made the rainbows.
Teacher:	That kind of fits the theory that the rainbow was made in the night.
Janelle:	Hey, I have a theory. When a rainbow is really small and disappears, she comes back at night, and she makes another one. She makes it bigger, and bigger, and bigger, until it goes all over the whole school!
Teacher:	So you think that when we come back to school tomorrow it's going to be bigger?
Many voices:	Yeah!
Zoe:	It's gonna go all the way around this room!
Livvy:	I would feel like a rainbow person!
Gigi:	When you touched the rainbow the colors went away.
Claire:	One time I stepped on a rainbow, but it was still there. It was not fading away. It was on my foot.
Zoe:	Hey, it's coming back! It's a different shape!
Livvy:	It looks like a glass bowl!
Holly:	Once I was watching a show, and I went into my dining room, and I saw lots of rainbows, and then I thought that I wanted to make a rainbow…so I got some water, and got a paper towel, and I put it in the sun, and it made a white rainbow, and I tried to show Mama, but she was trying to do something, so I didn't show her.
Teacher:	What's a white rainbow?
Olivia:	Was it on a white wall?
Holly:	You just put it on a paper towel to make it white. You need water.
Teacher:	Do we have water for this rainbow [on the wall]? No?
Minnie:	LOOK!!! TWO! (another rainbow had appeared on the wall).

Teacher: You might want to watch these rainbows today and see what they do.

After meeting Minnie decided to gather a posse to hunt for rainbows. Eventually, most of the children joined the hunt, documenting the rainbows they saw and announcing the actions of the rainbows. As they hunted for rainbows and documented their findings, the rainbow hunters co-constructed the theory that light was necessary for rainbow formation, so after a while, their hunt took on an organization of sorts, in all the places where light might be found.

Testing the "covering the rainbow" theory.

Hunting for rainbows where there is light, according to the children's developing theory.

The children documented their rainbow finds in different ways. Some drew rainbows. One documented the number of rainbows she found with tally marks. One child combined strategies, including a checkmark, a representation of a tree flower, and writing with her own alphabet, as well as drawings. I imagine she drew the tree flower (which the children had made previously using wire, beads, and silk flower parts), because she associated the colors of the tree flowers on display in the classroom with the colors of the rainbows.

The excitement lasted all morning.

Overheard:
Minnie: We need to hurry up and get all the rainbows. We have 5. We need 21! Guys, we're not going to give up!

Elizabeth: It has to be somewhere where the sun shines.

Conversation about the rainbows re-emerged at our last meeting when the rainbows were no longer visible.

Essie posed a theory: "Maybe the rainbow fairy catched them all up."

Someone picked up Essie's theory and suggested that the rainbow fairy took all the rainbows to her castle.

Over the years I must have participated in hundreds of conversations for the co-construction of theory. Some led to sustained research, and some did not. Regardless the children and teachers found value in the conversations themselves. The conversation above happened at the end of the first month of school with a class of children who, at first, rarely chose cooperative or collaborative engagement, nor did they participate in formal conversations. They taught me that the way to intellectual engagement, for them, was through imagination. The surprise and wonder of the rainbow experience made dialogue worth pursuing for them. Through that early conversation, the children discovered the excitement and pleasure of figuring things out together. Once they discovered the power of co-construction of theory to bring them together, they sought out dialogue and, eventually, collaboration on a larger scale.

Children can find conversations for the co-construction of theory or problem-solving quite satisfying. Once the children in my class experienced the pleasure of engaging in dialogue, our meetings would last much longer than I ever expected and much longer than I used to think possible with young children. They sustained them, not I. I was a participant but did much less talking than they did. Once children have the skills to engage, managing the conversation becomes more collaborative and democratic. Teachers *and* children ask for clarification from speakers. Anyone can challenge an idea or its consistency. Anyone can problematize. Anyone can suggest an idea (though it is rarely the teacher;

it is her job to learn about the children's intent, and she can't do that if she isn't listening). In my experience, the children were often loath to end good dialogue.

Stages of Participation in Group Conversations

When you first try to have group conversations with young children, they may not have learned that there can be pleasure in this kind of discourse. They may roll away from the group or play with their shoes or otherwise disengage. It's true that to engage in dialogue, children need to be able to articulate their ideas, and they need to have the disposition and skill to listen to each other. But we can't assume that just because a child is wiggling, she is not aware of the conversation around her. Look for evidence of engagement other than stillness and eye contact. If even a few children manage to get engaged, the non-present child likely will feel the interest and emotion of the others even if he isn't listening. Helping a child stay physically present in the vicinity of the conversation can lead to greater engagement over time. That may mean that you invite a child into your lap or to sit beside you, for example.

Just as children learn to read by reading, they learn to have good conversations by conversing. Before you initiate a class conversation, you will want to think about setting conditions conducive to participation. It helps to make sure that children are sitting so that they can see each other. In informal conversations, this happens naturally. But if you are having a conversation during a class meeting and the children are all sitting facing the teacher but with their backs to each other, it can be more difficult for them to engage.

When children participate in conversations, their disposition to engage in dialogue grows, as does their skill to do so. Your listening (with deep engagement) lends importance to the endeavor in the children's minds and serves as a model for how one participates in a conversation. In addition, you can use terms you hope the children will use on their own in conversation, such as, "Do you agree?" "What do you think?" "What is your theory?" and "Are you saying...?" The children will learn to say, "I agree/don't agree..." "I think..." "My theory is that..." "Are you saying ...?"

I have observed that the first step toward engagement during class conversation occurs when the child voluntarily joins the group, though he does not participate. He may not appear to be listening, but he is choosing to be with the group. At the next stage, he wants to participate in the conversation, but his comments may be off-topic. For example, if everyone is talking about birds, this child may say, "Last night, my daddy had to fix the sink." One step closer: he participates, and he is on topic, but all of his comments are repetitions of the comments of others. At another stage, he may articulate associations between the topic at hand and his own experiences or other previous knowledge. With experience, he begins to participate in conversation with opinions or hypotheses of his own. Finally, he is listening, engaged, articulates his theories, and begins to problematize. I'm not suggesting any kind of codified stage theory here. But it is important to acknowledge approximations toward participation. These early stages of engagement are explorations of participation. Over time children will share their ideas and interact with the ideas of others, and they will discover the power and pleasure of doing so. I'm not sure that you would arrive there without experiencing the earlier stages of engagement.

Consider this excerpt from a conversation, the second in a series. Emily has just welcomed a baby brother (Paul), and I noticed that the children were quite curious, not so much about the baby himself but about his experience before being born. I joined a conversation among a small group about the baby's pre-birth life to support the children's communication and to learn what meaning they were co-constructing about the baby inside the mommy. Determining that the ideas the children were articulating were compelling enough to support further dialogue, I analyzed the recording of the conversation in search of salient points. The next day I brought what I thought were the most prominent and intriguing ideas to the whole class: whatever happens to the mommy also happens to the baby; there are two pipes that connect the baby to the mommy, one for food and one for water; and when the baby comes out, "they" take the pipes out. When Naya proposed a theory at the beginning of the conversation, I took note. She had been trying to figure out how to participate in conversations, and this topic seemed to be compelling enough for her to pose her theories. She needed some support to hold her own with some highly motivated classmates. Notice my efforts to support her engagement.

> In her response my presentation of yesterday's theories, Renee clarified that the 'pipes' to which she referred yesterday were actually called cords (Renee has been thinking about this!). The children affirmed their belief that whatever happens to the mommy also happens to the baby and their theory about the pipes. And then they framed one of their questions in a new way: What happens to the baby inside the mommy (starting to take the perspective of the baby?).

Naya: The baby doesn't do the same thing (as the mother), because it's like in a bubble. There's like water outside of the mommy's tummy. The little baby has like a little bubble, and it's like a big air bubble.

Teacher: You think the baby's in an air bubble, and there's water outside the bubble inside the mommy?

Naya: Yes. First it got smaller, and then bigger, and then bigger, and then bigger till it be borned.

Teacher: And what happens to the bubble, Naya?

Gabby: The bubble pops!

Teacher: Do you agree, Naya?

Naya: No. It has a little crack. And then it gets more crack, and then it got born.

Teacher: So when it cracks then the baby is born?

Renee: Actually, the baby does everything that the mommy does, Naya, and if the baby was hungry and the mommy wasn't I think they would have to go to the doctor, and the doctor would take an x-ray of the baby and see if he really really was hungry. Then they would say the baby really is hungry. I'm going to give him some food, and they'd have to squirt in her body and make a tiny hole and put some medicine so she wouldn't feel it.

Teacher: Naya, do you agree that in the bubble the baby does everything the mommy does, or do you have a different idea?

Naya: I have a different idea. It just stays there and close their eyes till it's a little bit…if they see he or she feet it will just come out. When my brother's three I just got out.

Emily: I think the baby is inside an egg, and the egg is the size of the mommy's tummy, and then when it's about to be born it gets cracked, and when it's all cracked, it's born.

Teacher: Is that what happened to Paul?

Emily: I asked him at the hospital, and he said "Yes."

Renee: How does he talk?

Emily: He just…cries.

Notice, also, how, as the teacher in this conversation, I supported the conversation responsively and how my statements and questions affected the trajectory of the dialogue. Pay attention to what I didn't do, as well, for that is just as important to the conversation as what I said. You might notice the following:

- ◆ I made a point of referring to the children's comments.
- ◆ I acted as memory proxy, bringing the children's ideas back to them. For example, I brought the salient ideas, "whatever happens to the mommy also happens to the baby" and "there are two pipes connecting the mommy and the baby, one for food, and one for water"…back for more discussion.

- ♦ I *lent* a listening ear. That is, I supported the children in using their voices and in listening to each other. I didn't tell them to listen, nor did I listen for them but supplemented their efforts only as far as necessary.
- ♦ I kept the children's focus on each other. I always found it helpful to use body language, such as taking a physical listening stance myself or offering an open palm facing the speaker when children interrupted the speaker. When I reviewed videos of myself facilitating conversations with young children early in their experience, I noticed that I also used a lot of expression in my responses, sometimes showing the wonder or surprise or just intense interest that I imagined the children listening (*if* they were listening) might feel, in a way that I might not if I were having a conversation with my colleagues (though I don't know…you might ask them!).

Children's theories evolve from magical to logical over time. Conversations with peers in which children challenge each other's theories support that evolution. For example, say a group of children are expressing curiosity about how it rains. They articulate their theories in multiple languages, including verbally in class conversations. Their theories are magical in the beginning: "There is a giant machine in the sky that makes the water and fills the clouds until they leak," or "God and Santa Claus collaborate to make water from the air and then tell the wind to send the rain down," for example. These provisional theories are susceptible to challenges that arise in dialogue like "I disagree" or "But how can….?" Each child in a group may experience multiple challenges to his theories in the course of a conversation, making dialogue a conflict-rich opportunity for both intellectual and emotional growth. Over time, children's theories will evolve in sophistication whether you support good conversations or not, but meaningful dialogue does support that growth. In the meantime, the dynamic between magical and logical thinking is often fluid.

As children's skill in conversation grows, you will notice that they begin to problematize, especially if you have modeled it all along. To problematize is to challenge ideas in a conversation.

The language of problematizing might be, "But what if…" or "but that isn't what happened when…" When children begin to problematize during dialogue, you know they have achieved a level of engagement that is likely to sustain the conversation with less support from you. Problematizing takes a conversation beyond outpouring, where dialogue consists of a string of "what I know" statements, often disconnected from each other. It represents a new kind of flow in the conversation, where sequential ideas are connected to each other. It's a more articulate version of "I disagree," implying or stating the reason for disagreement.

To illustrate, here is an excerpt from a conversation we had in anticipation of a collaborative project with fifth graders in the school's Maker Space. Although our usual approach to supporting children's representation was to help them choose the materials most conducive to representing their idea, in this case, we were going from "choice of material" to "idea." The following is from a blog post about the experience. Children's problematizing comments are italicized:

> In Meeting this morning, we generated ideas for what could be made from plastic grocery bags, in preparation for working with the 5th graders in the Maker Space tomorrow. The children remembered their thoughts about the possibilities afforded by the materials from last week and posed theories about the feasibility of those plans. They also generated some new ideas to take to the Maker Space, where we will engage in conversation with the big girls about the possibilities.
>
> *The question:* What could you make by tying and weaving and connecting the bags together?
> *Julianna:* I was gonna make something that could stay outside. I was gonna make a swing set.
> *Teacher:* That you can swing on?
> *Helen:* Yes. I was going to make one for me to swing on, too.
> *Lola:* *Well, you can't make it. You need wood to make it.*

Julianna:	No you don't. You can weave. And then all you gotta do is tie plastic bags together to make the string.
Lola:	But when you sit on it it will tear!
T:	What would you have to do so it won't tear?
Lola:	You would have to [put] something hard on the bottom.

Reaching for clarity, I drew what I thought Julianna was describing on the whiteboard…a swing unsupported at the top… and asked what would happen if we sat on it. Lola said that it would tear, but Helen said it would fall "because it needs to be attached to something."

Helen:	Bags can't stand up. You need something that would stay steady and stand up.

Bags can't stand up on their side like that.

Cammie:	They would have to have something in them to make them stand up.
Julianna:	No. Bags can stay up like that.

Julianna draws her idea that a plastic bag can support a swing that can support a person.

Lola:	No, I don't think that would work, because it's just a bag. A bag can't hold things up.
Julianna:	It's gonna be tied.
Laura:	*The whole thing would tear and you might fall.*
Gabby:	To make a swing you're gonna need a plastic bag, then you're gonna take blocks, and you're gonna put it on the swing. Then you're gonna tie a plastic bag on a tree.

Gabby draws her thoughts about how one might make a swing with plastic bags.

Lola:	*But yours will rip, too, Gabby. I think that you can't make a swing out of plastic bags. Because if you sit on it they will all tear.*
Ada:	Actually, a good word is collapse.
Julianna:	*What if you took two weavings the same size and put them together and fill them with blocks? Then would it tear?*
Children:	No! Yes!

To encourage growth toward problematizing, you can model it, just as you might model listening and asking for clarification. That's it. It doesn't have to be taught directly. Like elements of other protocols, children adopt problematizing because they find it useful. For them, conversation is pleasurable. Therefore, they want to participate and don't want it to end. And so, they do what they have learned will keep the conversation going.

The Teacher as Curious Listener

I've worked with teachers who want to have good conversations with children but are not clear about their role, about how to allow/keep a conversation going, for example, and how much to get out of the children's way while supporting dialogue. They don't stray from their familiar control-the-conversation role. As a result, their conversations resemble call-and-response songs: the teacher asks, the children answer, the teacher tells, the children listen, and so on. It may feel familiar and safe to the teacher, but rarely do these conversations yield deep and reflective expression. The children are on a leash, so to speak, so we never witness the brilliance we might have if children were the primary participants in conversations.

The teacher's role in supporting good conversations with children is more about listening in a new way than about teaching children to converse. When you listen to children with all your senses and with an awake, curious mind, children understand that you are interested in what they have to say, and they are more inclined to try to articulate their point of view. They learn to listen to each other as you listen to them.

Listening is both disposition and action. Listening and curiosity travel together. If you are truly curious about children's theories, your responses will invite engagement on many levels. When young children ask questions, they are not always looking for you to provide an answer. Rather, they may be saying, "Think about this with me." They may even have a theory already and want to bounce it off someone they trust. That applies to the child who asks you, one-on-one, where the rainbow on the wall comes from. And it also applies to the child who asks the question in the context of group conversation. Only the child's imperative in that situation is, "Everyone here, think about this with me." He may want to share or test his theory out against the theories of others. The teacher who values children's engagement in meaningful conversation will approach the opportunity with the disposition to listen and not offer an answer to a declaration of wonder, and she will learn which of her actions do and do not tend to encourage children's sustained engagement and enjoyment.

You can only learn this if you listen. And you can't listen if you are talking. Your responses are born from your listening. It is both the source and the result of your curiosity: What are the children saying? The teachers I have worked with who have expressed frustration with class conversations often assume too quickly they know what children mean, and their responses reflect that haste. Better to set a goal to truly understand (and help the children understand) what speakers are saying than to have an agenda for the conversation. Often, young children are continuing to formulate their theories as they talk, so your questions to gain clarity can help speakers and listeners.

You will find that in the beginning, your role in conversation will be greater than it will be later once the children have experience with good conversations. To support that growth, ask questions you hope children will ask each other and themselves eventually. Questions like, "Do you mean____?" (clarifying), or "But earlier you said _____" or "But then why does _____ happen?" (challenging). Take the children's theories and ideas seriously and treat the children's theories and ideas with respect. Your goal is to understand and help the conversation continue, not to correct or say, "Actually, the truth is…." Giving children the "right" answer to a question with which they are happily struggling will often end their engagement in the conversation. When the conversation ends, so does the good thinking that happens during it. Set the primary goal: that children will get engaged and stay engaged for as long as they can in conversations about topics of interest to them.

Facilitating Conversation

I always try to facilitate conversations in as organic a way as possible. That is, in a way that approximates natural conversational rhythm as much as possible. I want every child to find and learn to use her voice in conversation. But I do not set contrived expectations like going round robin around the circle to achieve equitable participation. Instead, we all hear the ideas of those who have something to say, and I pay attention to those who have not spoken and make space for them to talk. For example, introverts are likely to take a bit more time formulating a response during conversation; it can be frustrating when, by the time you are ready to articulate your thoughts, the conversation has gone on without you. We want to support outspoken children to listen as well as talk and help the quiet ones get others' attention when they have something to say. With some children or around some topics, children may need a physical way to indicate they have something to say, like raising a hand. At first, the teacher may have to acknowledge the next speaker, but in time the children can manage the dialogue with less adult support. That is the goal. As soon as the children have internalized the Conversation Protocol and can sustain the conversation with less (or no) help, we should allow our participation to diminish. That is not to say that we don't participate at all. Rather, in time, the dialogue achieves a state of homeostasis where children are the primary actors and the teacher is a lesser participant. The responsive teacher is aware if she is participating more directly than is ideal, with an eye toward moving away from being the one who chooses the next speaker as soon as the children can take over that responsibility. In this way, we *lend* our control, but we don't bequeath it. Eventually, children learn to listen for a break in the conversation before they speak.

The strategies mentioned above, restating children's ideas, supporting listening with body language, expressing engagement in the conversation, and asking questions you hope children eventually will ask themselves, will all help maintain the flow of conversation. In addition, *not* doing some things can help children sustain interest in conversations, for example, not inserting your own agenda into the conversation or trying to make the conversation stick to the original topic. Consider letting the conversation choose its path. Conversations ramble, and some of the richest conversations I have ever had with children flowed from one topic to another related one, and so on until it landed on one that caught the children's imaginations well enough to support sustained interest. For example, the topic of a conversation that began as a meeting to help two children solve a social dilemma flowed from friendship to happiness to mysteries of human anatomy, where the children sustained it. The following excerpt begins at the point where the topic has shifted from friendship to happiness:

Teacher: What do you know about "happy?"
Melanie: You can hug somebody.
Teacher: Why is that happy?
Melanie: I love my mom a lot. When she's been on a trip, and she hugs me, that makes me happy when she comes back.
Helen: Well, happy isn't like you do something. It's like a feeling.
Lola (demonstrating the feeling): This is the best day of my life!

Crowd (everyone talking at once)

Amara: Like sometimes, when I'm good to my mommy that whole day, she's really happy, and she has a happy feeling.

Teacher:	She has a happy feeling. Where is that happy feeling?
Child:	In your brain.
Amara:	Happy feeling is in your heart.
Helen:	Probably your heart. Probably, if your feelings were in your brain, you wouldn't be able to think. All you'd be able to think about is your feelings.
Julianna:	Actually, I think in your brain. Because there's this thought that comes out, and it makes me really sad.
Amara:	If we have a field trip to the Science Museum, then we'll know where happiness comes from. If we go to the bone exhibit, we can see where happiness comes from…one day, Emmie and I went to the Science Museum, and I showed Emmie where all the parts of your body were, and I saw happiness in the brain.
Helen:	Actually, I changed my mind. I agree with Julianna.
Teacher:	*So, then, Helen, is there room for feelings and for thoughts in your brain, do you think? (Yes)*
Lola:	Not really. Because if all your thoughts were in your brain…All of them were in your brain…you wouldn't be able to think of anything. So, if I had all these thoughts in my brain right now, I wouldn't even be able to come up with any words or ideas to solve things.
Amara:	I disagree. At the Science Museum, it does have happy thoughts in your brain.
Lola:	But maybe they're just using their imagination.
Amara:	They're not. Everything there is for real that happened.
Teacher:	*Ada, where do you think happy is?*
Ada:	In your heart.
Nora:	Cause God's in your heart.
Maeve:	No, God is in your body.
Nora:	Your heart and your body.
Lola:	My dog that died is still in my heart. He went up to Heaven, but he's still in my heart because God's in my heart, and God is the same as dogs, but God's more special than dogs.

Teacher:	*Cammie, where do you think happy is?*
Cammie:	I think it comes from your heart. Because your heart is shaped like a heart.
Lindsey:	No. Your heart is meat, but not shaped like a heart.
Amara:	No, 'cause then you'll have to be eating it!
Lindsey:	You can't eat your heart because it's meat. You need it to live.
Lola:	Cause your heart can live…without dying, it doesn't need food. It's still going to be inside of us, even when we're in Heaven.
Maeve:	Your heart is for your brain to get smart.
Amara:	No, your brain is for your heart to get smart.
Lola:	But our hearts are the specialest. Our hearts are specialer than our brain. Because God's in them.
Helen:	And, because your brain doesn't keep you living. Your heart keeps you living.
Teacher:	*Could you live without your brain?*
Amara:	You can live without your brain, but you just can't think good without your brain.
Lola:	No, it would be really squishy right here (pointing to her head) and you won't have any bones.

Crowd

Julianna:	You can't live without *both*. Cause your head piece is one piece. You can never get squishy over here (pointing to her head and face). Your head is one piece. And you can't live without your head.

Not every class conversation leads to something profound. But many profound conversations begin with a banal observation. Similarly, every beautiful conversation does not result in a big research project. There's much to learn for children and teachers from a single rich conversation. The thinking teacher, who is constantly assessing what's going on in the classroom and asking herself, "What's being learned here?" also asks herself what there is to be learned about the children, learning, and teaching from engaging in class and small group conversations. Good conversations and our documentation of them can be our teachers if we let them.

There will be times when dialogue falters. Having good conversations with children is an art and can't be regulated by a script. In a way, the teacher's role here is improvisational. Like improv, it depends on a "Yes…and" mindset; there is no knowing where a conversation will go, and that's the beauty of it. The thinking teacher will ride the wave of the conversation's own rhythm, and that includes having a bit of grace when, inevitably, she says something that halts a conversation instead of sustains it or tries too hard, and suddenly the dialogue is in her court and not in that of the children. I can't tell you how many times, especially when I was new to the process, I had to shrug and move on when a conversation faltered because of me, knowing that if the topic really was compelling for the children, it would arise again.

"Incorrect" Theories

The curious, listening teacher will respond to children's thinking and won't worry about accuracy. When considering children's theories about how the world works, it is more important that their thinking grows more reasoned, for example, than that they have their facts right. If you correct their theories, if you say, "Well, actually, here's the way it is," the children will have no reason to remain in dialogue. The conversation will end. And if children become accustomed to your role as answer-giver in this way, you will have a hard time engaging them in conversation that leads to co-construction of theory at all. So, you don't want to correct their theories. But you do want to respond to the theory a child is proposing. For example, if a child were to attribute the source of snow to God and a snow machine, though you know the theory is neither logical nor "true," rather than thinking about what he does not know, you might consider what he is showing that he does know. He is giving you a window into his understanding of cause and effect; that snow must be "made," somehow, and doesn't just "appear"; and even that he believes the theory that God makes the snow is not enough so the child added a machine to his theory. You will want to hear what the children say and respond with a mind toward helping them sustain the dialogue that is the path to intellectual growth. Anything you do to interrupt the flow of the children's co-construction of theory, like telling them "the answer" to their research question, will interrupt the deep thought process that primes further inquiry. So don't worry that you are doing them a disservice by facilitating conversations for the co-construction of theory for as long as the children are interested, regardless of facts and reality.

You needn't worry that those provisional theories will persist. As children's capacities grow, old theories tend to no longer be satisfying. It is my experience that if they have engaged in sustained research about a topic, with many conversations and with representation of the project's ideas in multiple languages, children create a lasting mental space for the topic. They tend to notice and accommodate any new information that they encounter about the subject long after the investigation ends. If that happens when they are in a different cognitive developmental stage, they will consider their old theories no longer adequate. Because their earlier study "primed" their curiosity long-term, they are more likely to re-engage with the topic. I have known children, having "finished" a long-term research project, to relaunch some version of the project much later when they encountered a new fact or event related to the original research topic. For example, out of the blue, months after an investigation about stars ended, one child said to her classmates, "Remember when we were talking about stars? Well, my dad read me this book that said the stars were fire," which inspired more conversation and representation about a topic we adults thought was dormant. Sustained curiosity about a topic they studied previously is one of the great benefits of long-term research projects. Conversations for the co-construction of theory play a significant role in those projects and in children's continued curiosity.

Developing a Culture of Conversation

In the beginning, the teacher may initiate and facilitate class conversations based on the informal dialogue she witnesses. It is through participation in these experiences that children discover the power and pleasure of dialogue. In time, conversations for co-construction of theory or plans become part of children's way of being together. They suggest topics for class meetings. They include plans for dialogue when they encounter problems. They create a culture of conversation. When children in a group have developed a culture of conversation, they hold certain expectations of dialogue.

- They expect to solve problems through conversation.
- They expect to find pleasure in dialogue.
- They expect to be able to call a meeting and have a conversation when there is something to figure out.
- They expect that their voices will be heard and that their teacher will support others to listen.
- They expect that conversation will be useful to them personally.

Once a culture of conversation develops, children understand its power and not only participate actively in conversation for the co-construction of theory but also often initiate conversations when wonders arise. During a cognitive argument, for example, children who understand the power of conversation for the co-construction of theory may say, "Let's call a meeting!"

For children to experience pleasure in these conversations, they must perceive the exchange as providing both a social connection and a path to understanding. Such conversations cannot be contrived. They must be about real curiosity, real problems, and topics of real interest to the children. Where some pedagogical approaches fail is that the topics of conversation come only from the teacher (and often not at all about her curiosity about the children and their interests) or, worse, from a canned curriculum. The Conversation Protocol is organic and dynamic and cannot be predetermined by anyone. It is co-constructed in

Once a culture of conversation develops, children know that they can call meetings to discuss disagreements.

real time by teachers and students. The protocol offers guidance in accomplishing a culture of conversation, the teacher's role in having good conversations, keeping conversations going, embracing cognitive conflict in conversations, and more.

The Conversation Protocol

What if you have never facilitated this kind of conversation with young children? How do you begin? If you don't have experience having conversations with young children, or those you have had have not been particularly satisfying, consider starting with a small group. The group should be big enough that there are enough voices and opinions to keep the conversation going.

You might start by listening to children's spontaneous conversations as they play. When you catch a conversation between or among children, record it or take notes. Review your traces of the conversation and ask yourself: What is the children's intent? Do the participants seem to be trying to figure something out? Might this be a conversation for the co-construction of theory about how the world works? Are the children expressing a theory or something they know or have experienced? Or does it seem to be about keeping the relationship going? Like a "me, too" type of conversation? Of course, there are myriad possibilities. What is important is that you listen to this conversation with curiosity. Don't assume too quickly you know what the children mean. Once you've practiced this kind of listening for a while, you can focus your listening a bit and orient toward ideas that could be the seeds of larger conversations.

When you recognize or create a provocation that you think might support children's engagement, lend it importance by sitting down with the children, eye to eye. and taking the stance, "tell me more." Then listen. I got in the habit of turning on the voice recording app on my phone every time we sat down to talk. Sometimes nothing interesting happened, and I just erased the recording. But sometimes...and I could never predict when... something wonderful emerged from an everyday conversation. Having the recording allowed me to transcribe and study it for points that seemed to be intriguing, emotional, or significant in some way. I then had something to bring back to the children, to poke the idea a bit.

In the second conversation on that same topic, to which you are bringing the salient points/theories from earlier dialogue, remind the children of the context of the original conversation and just read their comments to them. If the children's theories are still of interest to them, the conversation should start itself. Your job is to keep the integrity of the conversation intact for as long as the children are interested. If it has to be interrupted, for example, for an appointment the children have elsewhere, let them know that the dialogue can continue later, and you will remind them where they left off. Having a recording will allow you to do this.

Every conversation starts with a provocation. It might be one child's provocative statement, a naturally occurring event, a mystery that has emerged in the classroom, or an idea the teacher brings to the children inspired by their play. The provocation might be conflicting theories of two or more children. It might be a provocation that the classroom environment has produced. It might be a hypothesis the teacher has made about children's intent through studying her documentation of play...just to name a few possibilities. Here are examples of some conversation provocations.

Conflicting Theories
David brought a cotton boll he collected on a trip with his family to show his friends. He told a group of interested classmates that he had seen cotton growing in a field. Kali doubted that and said, "You can't grow cotton." The teacher thought Kali's theory was interesting and brought the interchange to the class meeting.

Environmental Provocations
The school's janitor came to talk to the teacher about some evidence of mice in the old building. Visitors to the classroom were always interesting to the children, so they heard a part of the adult conversation, and when the janitor left, they started wondering aloud.

Kimmy: Maybe we can see the mice.
Teacher: How could we see the mice, Kimmy?
Jasmine: If they're scared of us.
Children: I know! I know!

The children's passionate reply was the provocation for many more class conversations and a sustained research project to catch and see the mice. They never did catch any mice. But they did adopt a kitten to scare the mice out into the open, sculpted a life-sized clay model of the kitten so she would remember what she looked like when she knew the children, and, curious about what was inside the kitten, engaged in research about the anatomy of a cat. In this case, the unseen mice were the provocation for a conversation, and the conversation was a provocation for a long-term investigation.

Documented Play

When a teacher observes that one compelling idea keeps coming up in play with passion and contagion, she may initiate a conversation either with the small group of players or with the whole class. She wants to understand what is behind the passion, repetition, and contagion, and she wants to know how she can support the children in understanding what it is that they are exploring through play. The play is a provocation for conversations, which are provocations for future provocations.

The Protocol

When calling upon the Conversation Protocol:

- Listen for and record children's spontaneous conversations. If you see possibilities for further engagement with the topic, transcribe the conversation.
- Study the transcript to get insight into the children's intent. Look for seeds of possibility for further conversation.
- Bring salient ideas back to the children in a small or large group.
- Listen actively:
  - Model a listening stance.
  - Restate children's comments to clarify or help children hear what another has said.
  - Ask clarifying questions.
  - Challenge ideas when appropriate.
  - Problematize when appropriate.
- Help children focus on each other, using your body language.
- Go with the flow:
  - Don't correct misconceptions.
  - Allow children to challenge each other.
- Bring a small group's thinking to the whole group for inspiration and/or relaunch.
- Act as memory proxy.

Consider This

- How do the children in your class view meeting times? As an experiment, have one adult facilitate the meeting and another take note of the children's body language and activity. What engages them? How often do adults redirect children's bodies and voices? How much time is spent disengaged? Consider: whose meeting is this?
- Have a conversation with either a small group or the whole class. Bring an idea you have heard children talk about or an idea from their play. Choose an idea you expect will support dialogue. Set up the meeting so that the children can see each other. If they are on the floor, sit on the floor with them. Have a tape recorder or recording app ready. Then ask, "Tell me about____." Afterward, transcribe and study the conversation. What did you learn? Is there anything you would do differently next time?
- When you are observing children's play, make guesses about what their deeper meaning might be. Record all the possibilities (this is best if you can do it with a colleague). Don't do anything about it yet. Observe some more, with a list in hand (or in memory). Does the children's subsequent play support some of your guesses? Make a new list but keep the old one. How does your impression of the children's intent change over time?

Reference

Forman, G. (2014). "Reflections on *Tenderness – The Story of Laura and Daniele.*" *Innovations in Early Education: The International Reggio Emilia Exchange*, 21(3), 29.

9

Flow Challenge

Cognitive Conflict in Play and Conversation

Children will disagree in play or conversation. How we respond can determine how those moments contribute to the their intellectual and emotional growth. If we avoid cognitive conflict in the classroom, we are missing a great resource for learning. Some of the best learning happens in the stew of cognitive conflict, where ideas collide, and we face opinions and information that challenge our understanding.

What follows is a conversation a group of five-year-olds and their teacher had, beginning with a knock-knock joke at the snack table.

What Do the Mornings Do When It's Night?

At the snack table with friends and a teacher one day, Brook said, 'Knock, knock.'

'Who's there?' the teacher responded.

'What do the mornings do when it's night?'

'What?'

'They die.'

The children in Brook's class had developed a culture of conversation with each other, and the knock-knock joke slid easily into a brief conversation among those at the table.

Brook: There are new mornings each day. The morning sun never dies.

Evie: No. It's always the same sun.

Brook: The sun's children are the mornings. They grow up in the daytime. The moon's children are the nights. Their birthdays are at night.

Molly: The morning just goes away because the sun is away from the earth. The moon comes closer to the earth.

Teacher: What makes that happen?

Ella: The sun comes closer. That's Molly's theory. But I agree with Brook's theory.

The rhythm of eating snack interrupted the flow of the conversation, but the teacher thought the ideas were intriguing, so she asked the children if they'd like to take their ideas to the whole class for discussion. They agreed enthusiastically. Later, when the class gathered, the children who participated in the snack table conversation reiterated their theories, helped by the teacher, who was acting as memory proxy.

Elise: No, no. It goes to like another country. The sun does.

Brook: And she takes her children, the mornings, with her.

Elise: No. Suns don't have children. The sun just moves to like another country. The sun can move to Germany.

Child: Or China!

Teacher: How does the sun know where to go?

Molly (being silly): It has a car!

Elise (quite seriously): No. There's no cars for suns.

Teacher: How does the sun know where to go?

Evie: Maybe he just goes wherever he wants to.

Teacher: So you think the sun goes somewhere different every morning?

Children:	No!
Teacher:	Does the sun always come here every morning? Yes? So, if the sun knows to come here every morning does it know where to go at night?

There arose a tentative "yes" from a few.

Mariah:	That's because the sun is not real.
Children:	It is.
Mariah:	I mean it's not real...with a mouth, nose, and mouth.
Teacher:	Are you saying the sun is not a person? Yes? Is the sun real? Yes? Do you all agree?
Elise:	The sun is in outer space.
Molly:	Wait! But the sun is the closest planet to our earth.
Georgia:	The sun is just a huge ball of fire. That's all it is.
Ella:	Hot lava!
Georgia:	Not hot lava. Just fire.
Holly:	The sun is the biggest, brightest star.
Georgia:	Then why does it come out in day?
Evie:	It's the only star in the day.
Holly:	My mommy says it's the brightest.
Brook:	And it runs out of gas at night.
Elise:	It just goes to somewhere else.
Children:	No! No, it doesn't! (apparently this is not plausible)

This conversation is, in a way, a dance between imagination and 'fact.' Mediating the dance is reason...intellect. Not all the 'facts' the children have heard and can repeat make sense to them. And so, they struggle to make meaning, reaching for the plausible.

Peyton:	Well, I think, the sun...you can't see it when it's nighttime on our planet, Earth, but it still shines in outer space.

Teacher:	So it still is shining in outer space, and no one can see it at night? Well, that's different from Elise's theory which is that the sun goes somewhere else at night. You think no one can see it at night?
Peyton:	No. Some people can see it. When it's nighttime it still shines in outer space. But then it's morning in China, too. At the same time.
Molly:	Some places, our night is their day, and our day is their night.
Elise:	Well, when we have daytime Germany is nighttime right now…when it's daytime for us.
Molly:	It's the same thing in Russia.
Mariah:	The same thing in everywhere.
Peyton:	When it's our day it shines in outer space AND in our country. And when it's our night and China's day then the sun shines in outer space, and it shines on China.
Teacher:	OK, well, how does it do that? How does it get from one place to another?
Georgia:	It stays in outer space. The sun turns around to China, and it's still shining in outer space.
Teacher:	Does it have a shiny side and a not shiny side?
Molly:	Well, sometimes at China there can be places where it's dark, like in a prison or something.
Georgia:	Like dungeons.
Elise:	The sun is all bright.
Teacher:	All bright, Elise says. There's no dark side.
Molly:	The sun is always moving. Our planets are always moving.
Evie:	The sun is not a planet. It just goes wherever it goes.
Teacher:	How does it go?
Evie:	I don't know.
Molly:	'Cause we don't live in outer space.
Many voices:	Yes we do! No we don't!
Molly:	We live on a planet in outer space. We don't live in outer space. We live on a planet in outer space.
Evie:	We live on the earth! It's a planet!

Elise:	One planet went away from earth.
Molly:	Yeah! There's one planet that got lost!
Evie:	There's one planet that got lost, and that planet is Pluto.
Peyton:	Did it go to the black hole?
Elise:	No. It got lost.
Teacher:	How does a planet get lost?
Molly:	I don't know. But Pluto got lost and it's not a planet anymore.
Teacher:	Is that because it got lost, or did it get lost because it wasn't a planet anymore?
Molly:	It just got lost. And now it's not a planet anymore.
Evie:	But no planet can ever get lost at space.
Teacher:	Why, Evie?
Evie:	Because the planet Pluto…the special parts of space are the places around the world, so…there's not really aliens up there, but some say [there are], so maybe the planet got chased away by aliens. Some people don't think aliens are fake. They believe they're real.
Holly:	My Papa believes in aliens.
Teacher:	Do you believe that aliens chased Pluto away?
Molly:	No.
Holly:	I kind of believe in aliens. Because no one's ever seen an alien, so it's kind of a mystery.
Teacher:	Because no one knows for sure?
Ella:	We should go in a spaceship and find out!

This conversation was rich with conflicting views, and it was this diversity of perspective that inspired enthusiasm. As a result, this wasn't the end of the children's engagement with the topic. Because they had come to see conversations for the co-construction of theory or for planning as pleasurable, it wasn't unusual for the children to stay engaged with conversations for long periods. The teacher intentionally supported the culture of conversation and the growth of children's expectation that conversations are valuable.

Conflict in Conversation

Like "good trouble," there is good cognitive conflict (confronto), where children disagree with each other and articulate why. Some of the best learning happens in the stew of cognitive conflict, where ideas collide, and we face opinions and information that challenge our understanding. However, if people take umbrage when someone disagrees with them, and feelings get hurt and loom large, it becomes impossible to think and dialogue may fall apart. You can help children ride this wave. Framing dissenting opinions by asking, "You don't agree?" and asking the child whose theory was challenged, "What do you think about that?" can keep disagreement in the cognitive realm. Honoring all opinions/theories and helping children see them as possibilities helps as well. We want to be careful to avoid saying, "Well, actually, here's the way it really is," or telling one child he's right. That will be sure to take the wind out of the conversation! Help children exercise flexibility of thinking and emotional flexibility, which we all need if we are to consider the perspectives of others. Help them move toward curiosity and away from becoming too attached to their own opinions. Your calm demeanor, focused interest in the dialogue, and effort to keep the conversation in the intellectual realm will also help to sustain the conversation for as long as the children are interested.

Developing a language for disagreement can be worthwhile. During conversations with children, you can use expressions that you expect they will find useful in conversation, such as, "Do you agree?", "You disagree. What is your theory?", "Do you have a theory?" or "What do you think?" These words imply that differing opinions are good and expected in conversation. In time, you will notice that the children begin to use that language to regulate cognitive conflict on their own. You can also model ways of listening with your body, sitting at the children's level and leaning in. If there are interrupters, it can help to present your open palm to the speaker as an invitation to continue and to remind listeners of their role without breaking the flow of the conversation.

It's a Crowd!

Conversation is a collaborative venture. It can't happen without multitudes. Sometimes in a class conversation, when emotions rise and everyone talks at once, a teacher might be tempted to consider it unruly or as a loss of control. She might, quite rightly, consider it conflict. With a bit of a mind shift, you can help such passion support sustained dialogue rather than derail it. Old scripts would tell you to halt the conversation, remind the children to talk one at a time, and set up control systems like round-robin turn-taking. But the passion behind the crowd is emotion that can bind children to the idea(s) at hand. The children's emotional relationship with the idea encourages deep engagement, so we don't want the crowd to end the conversation. It's better to acknowledge the passion: "Wow, you have a lot to say! Let's hear what everyone thinks," and then relaunch the conversation by reiterating what the last speaker said.

Every year, the first time a crowd emerged in a class conversation, we would talk about it as we did any problem to solve. "Oh my, what just happened?" I might begin. Everyone perceived that it was difficult to continue when many children talked at once. I asked them what they thought we should do if there was a crowd in a conversation. Of course, in different years, there were different (though similar) solutions. But every year after we had that initial conversation, all anyone had to do was say, "It's a crowd!" and the children would regroup, knowing that everyone had a voice and would have a chance to use it. In time, the children managed those moments more and more among them, announcing the crowd themselves and re-grouping for continued dialogue.

Difficult Topics in Conversation

Teachers may feel conflicted when children bring up difficult topics in conversation. "Should I allow this conversation?" they may ask themselves. "Do I dare?" Following children into awkward or controversial topics can feel risky. We need a certain degree of confidence in our ability to have conversations with children, particularly if we're worried about where the topic might take us. In order to find the courage to have conversations about difficult subjects, we need to develop a disposition toward taking certain risks. Perhaps it helps to ask, "What am I worried will happen?" And then, "What is there to gain?" There's a gift in dialogue about difficult topics. Significant questions ...ideas that have challenged humankind forever... are as compelling for children as they are for adults, and the children's engagement bears this out. Can the insight we get from joining children as they tackle the mysteries of life lend us courage? Emotion-laden topics like death and controversial ones like theology can be some of the most fertile ground for dialogue, listening, and good thinking precisely because of the affect they inspire. I have long held that there's a particular reciprocity between emotion and intellect and have known groups of children who first began to engage in cognitive dialogue *because* the topic inspired emotional engagement. "We don't talk about that here" are limiting words that I believe should never be used without considering what might be lost for the sake of maintaining adults' comfort zones.

As an example, I offer you the story of the dead fish, first published in a blog post at pokenwright.com.

> One morning, we entered the classroom to find that the Betta fish we'd had for about a month had died. The children never paid the sickly fish much attention...until that day. Some of the children were distressed, and others were full of questions, but everyone was interested.
>
> We decided to hold a community meeting (two classes, 23 children, ages four to five and a half) to unpack the children's thoughts and feelings about the fish's demise. These excerpts from their dialogue include assertions direct from parents or Sunday school. But there are also theories about how death and dying work, some philosophy, and some theology, evidence that young children

can and do engage in deep and meaningful dialogue about important matters.

Some topics are particularly difficult for adults but are fertile ground for co-construction and deep discussion for children. We could have simply 'disappeared' the dead fish. Considering their lack of engagement with the little guy while he was alive, I rather doubt anyone would have cared. But then we would have missed an opportunity to invite the kind of dialogue that comes out of deep engagement and emotion. Follow the conversation below and see if you agree.

AB:	I haded a fish, his name was Junior Ray and after my grandparents went in Heaven, my fish went in Heaven.
Teacher:	Your fish went in Heaven! Do you think our fish is in Heaven?
Many voices:	Yes! No!
GT:	His bones are.
HR:	My mom says once you bury an animal, then God picks it up from the dirt and then his whole body is just stuck in the dirt, and then when the fish gets to Heaven it gets a whole 'nother new body. That's what my mom said.
Teacher:	So what part of him goes up there if it's not his body?
HR:	Well, the old part of like the bones and the skin would just be buried in the dirt, and then…he goes up in Heaven and gets a whole new body. Like the same kind of body, except never dying again.
Teacher:	Can you only die once? (Yes)
BS:	One day I saw a dead kind of bird…and we took good care of it…and he didn't come alive again.
Teacher:	Are you saying that our fish will not get a new body?

HR:	He will get a new body. Because God can do a lot of things that we can't do.
BeS:	Well, your bones go to Heaven and your skin doesn't.
GT:	When any kind of animal dies they get buried and their spirits go up to Heaven.
Teacher:	So what part gets buried then?
GT:	Their body and their spirit goes up.
Teacher:	What is the spirit of a fish like?
GT:	It's a fish, except it's invisible and it's not a real fish.
Teacher:	So let me ask you this. Is our fish's spirit already up in Heaven?
GT:	It might take a long time to go up to Heaven.
HR:	No. No. God always has a way for something good.
Teacher:	What way would God have to make this good?
HR:	Well, God's arms are so large He can lift the fish up to Heaven.
ML:	Did you know that my Daddy knows everything in the whole wide world that some people don't know, even my friend Amory, that is not in this class. He didn't read the Bible, he just knows that if you go up to Heaven, your skin just lays on the floor, and my dog already died.
Teacher:	Did his skin lie on the floor?
ML:	No. He was just gone. To Heaven.
SK:	You know what? When my fish died named Goldie, I got a new fish on my birthday. Goldie just died and we threw him in the toilet.
Teacher:	Did his spirit go in the toilet, too?
SK:	Yeah. He went to Heaven.
BeS:	No. No. [The toilet] leads to the ocean.
ML:	No, that leads to the sewer. Then he'll get eaten by a crocodile.

HG:	No, he'll come out into the wild world around us.
Teacher:	Can we watch the fish go into Heaven?
KS:	God won't do it if you're watching.
SH:	Yeah. God's invisible.
GT:	He's giant.
ML:	God doesn't even exist!
EG:	God does exist.
GT:	God is giant, because He's holding the world in his hands, and the world is really big.
KS:	The world comes down with Him to find the fish buried. He takes the fish from the hole…
HR:	No, no, K____, that's not right. We live on a planet called Earth, and God's holding it, and it can't be that God lives in outer space. That's impossible.
KS:	Maybe, if God holds the Earth like this, it might fall out of His hands.

The children discussed how they thought God positions his hands to hold the Earth. They continue.

EG:	We never know. I think God lives in Outer Space. God could be invisible.
SK:	And what if He lived right over here, and God was walking over the whole world, and He found Heaven. Heaven is a long way.
ML:	God would have to just walk and walk and walk one hundred and a gazillion walk times to get to the Earth.
MH:	We might seem a little big, but my brother told me that we're actually very small. The Earth is really small.
CP:	No. The world is BIG!
BS:	Actually, the sun is bigger than the Earth.
SH:	You'll see if you go into Outer Space. And you'll see that we are not people. We are sheep. We're God's sheep.
GT:	Cause He's watching over like shepherds watch over their sheep.

HG:	Do you know persons can be animals?
MH:	People are animals.
GT:	We're a type of animal.
AT:	Well, how could God go down to get the fish if He is holding the world?
GT:	Cause the fish is floating. And then He has magic, and He could make the world float and then He could go down and get the fish.
AT:	He could hold the world with one hand and then use the other hand to get the fish. I have one more word to say. If the astronauts go into Space, if he didn't see God, who would hold the globe?
Child:	He's invisible!
SC:	God lives in Heaven.
Teacher:	Not in space? (No)
GT:	Heaven is a type of planet.
BS:	God remembers [reminds] me of the invisible cat in *Alice in Wonderland* because He's invisible.
BeS:	God is not invisible. He lives far away from Space.

I never went looking for uncomfortable topics for conversation. They emerged as children experienced and thought about the world. Some of the richest, deepest conversations I have had with young children were about ideas adults find awkward. To allow children to explore these ideas fully, we may have to sit with our own inner conflict. As educators, we also must stay in dialogue with parents and guardians so that they understand that we are not teaching children about these huge ideas but listening. I chose the class blog as my communication tool; you may have a different platform for parent participation. In the blog, I would present excerpts from the children's conversations, along with my interpretation, which was always neutral if there were two different sides to an issue. I also articulated what I thought the significance of the conversation was for the children at the time. What were they trying to understand? How did they hear their families' voices as they articulated their opinions? In the dead fish conversation, the children retained the words of parents or Sunday School, but they had constructed their own theory around those words, which was probably not what the parents thought their children understood. Because we offered transparency, sensitivity, and interpretation that privileged the thinking of the child, we found that parents appreciated knowing how their children were thinking. Most shared our curiosity about children's perspectives on difficult topics. As a result, home-school conflict was not an issue.

Cognitive Conflict

Cognitive conflict can take the form of verbal arguments around ideas, plans, or theories. Disagreements that happen in play, in research, and in conversation are vital to the learning process. The perspective of the other is information that may challenge our current understanding. Without challenge, an oyster doesn't make a pearl, and we would be relegated to live only with what we already know. When someone else's perspective is different from ours we have four choices: ignore it (which happens if it's too far from what we understand); accommodate it, expanding our current understanding (if it's close to what we already understand); argue with it internally; or argue with it externally. We may not accommodate new information that opposes what we think we know right away. Our first response may be to argue. But if we can listen with an open mind, the new information pokes at our understanding. We may mull it over and then become more aware when we hear similar information around us. What we know and what we've heard may wrestle a bit, but in the end, we have a new understanding that accommodates the new information or that we have constructed using both old understanding and new information.

When visiting the schools in Reggio Emilia I am always intrigued by how much teachers and learners seem to enjoy cognitive conflict and how different that feels from observing cognitive conflict in the US. Here, children and adults sometimes seem offended when faced with a point of view different from their own. But what if we welcomed those differences in perspective, culture, opinion, and lived experience? When we interact only with those whose experiences and opinions are similar to our own, we struggle to grow. We lose the opportunity to develop the flexibility of thinking that good conflict can exercise, and our world can become small. In fact, we see this very thing happening now in our divided nation. We seem to have an inability to have cognitive conflict without emotional conflict. This divisiveness makes the role of educators both different from before and of utmost importance. Can we help the citizens of our country prevent the loss of our cognitive flexibility and self-imposed insulation through the education we offer?

Having good conversations with children is an excellent way to invite cognitive conflict for good. When we engage in dialogue with children, we help them find their voice, grow their ability to listen, take the perspective of the other, and accommodate worthy theories of the other into their own thinking. Many teachers struggle to have such conversations with young children, however. It is, indeed, an art. But it's an art that the Conversation Protocol can support. As you use the protocol and a culture of conversation develops among the children, and as they discover the power and pleasure of dialogue, children will seek out the protocol when they find themselves in cognitive conflict.

Consider This

What is your usual response when children in a meeting

- ♦ Interrupt each other?
- ♦ All talk at once?
- ♦ Tell each other they disagree?
- ♦ Bring up a controversial topic?

Do you feel any different about these situations after reading the last two chapters?

10

Flow Challenge
The Project Stalls

When an investigation stalls or never gets off the ground, the thinking teacher asks why. To identify the reason is his research about the children's research, and the possibilities are many. Perhaps the subject isn't compelling enough for the children. Perhaps the children haven't had enough experience with group communication to co-construct a way forward through conversation. Or enough experience with collaboration. Or with the materials they have chosen to use to represent their ideas. Perhaps the children need additional tools or techniques to realize their intent. Perhaps they need support to develop a shared vision of what they are trying to do. Any one of these sticking points can prevent or derail a research project. There can be no ready-made scripts to address these issues, for everything depends on your answer to your why. But the Investigation Protocol can both give insight into that "why" and offer a scaffold for getting unstuck.

The Investigation Protocol

One of the gifts the educators in Reggio Emilia have given us is a new understanding of the value of sustained research with children. Two of the primary goals of children's research are that the children come to understand and realize their intent and that they choose to pursue that intent. And, with sustained engagement, their understanding and personal growth reaches as far and goes as deep as possible. Contrast this with traditional pedagogy in which it is the teacher's well-meaning intent that matters. That teacher says, "We are studying space, and these are the concepts we will cover." She decides ahead of time when the project will begin and when it will end. The traditional teacher decides on the scope of the teaching (I will not say the scope of the learning, because this teacher's approach emphasizes teaching. The learning is assumed.). I learned from my years of engaging with children and their research that the scope of children's learning through research was far greater than I would ever have planned. The learning is vast, and the trajectory is often unpredictable. There can be no how-to manual that imbues children's research with certainty. The Investigation Protocol is for teachers who seek procedural and/or emotional support to start or continue to engage in children's research. It is a guide for a teacher's thinking as she works collaboratively with the children on research projects they navigate together. It's a set of strategies and stances that she might take when a question or topic arises that holds possibilities for significant investigation. Here are the elements of the protocol:

- Create a rich, inspiring environment and observe/document what children do in it.
- Recognize a compelling idea or question for research.
- Ask yourself if the idea might be significant enough to sustain collaborative research. If so:
- Document the children's interactions with that idea. Continue to document as the research progresses.
- Offer a provocation (an invitation to interact with the idea) to test a hypothesis about children's intent or as an invitation to engage/re-engage with the idea.
- Observe the children's responses to the provocation.
- Work with small groups to realize their intent.
- Bring the small groups' progress back to the whole group periodically.
- Be aware of opportunities to "relaunch" an investigation.

Keep reading to learn more about each element of the Investigation Protocol.

The Environment

Create a rich, inspiring environment and observe/document what children do in it. Research with and about young children begins with your observations in an environment curated to encourage participation, collaboration, curiosity, creativity, and inquiry. The environment must invite a response from the children that will show you who they are. A learning environment that invites children to be active participants in their own learning is an essential condition for children's authentic expression and learning, which are what teacher-researchers need if we are to study children, learning, and teaching.

As you observe the children's interactions in and with the environment, document and mine your documentation for signs of passion, contagion, energy, and repetition in the children's play, conversation, and representation. When you observe an idea that is repeated, contagious, and emotionally energized, you may hypothesize that it is a compelling one for the children. Hold that hypothesis for a bit as you continue to observe. As you do, the idea will begin to reshape the lens with which you observe the children. If your hypothesis is confirmed through continued observation, you may ask yourself what about the topic seems to hold the greatest interest for them.

The Idea

Recognize a compelling idea or question for research. Perhaps the same idea comes up in children's play, representation, and/or conversation over and over. Or you notice that every class conversation seems to suction to that idea over several days. Or that the children's dramatic play is about variations on a theme repeatedly.

You might perceive a certain passion in the children's conversation about the idea. Maybe everyone talks at once in excitement. Perhaps you notice that whenever the idea is being represented in play, conversation, or representation, the emotional timbre seems to click up a notch. Whether the topic emerges from children's expression, from a naturally occurring event, or from the teacher's curiosity about an aspect of teaching and learning, the children's emotional response to it (passion, repeated engagement, and/or contagion) is an indication that the idea is a compelling one for them.

You might notice that an idea seems to live in the ether. For example, a group of children are deeply engaged in making a river in the sandbox outdoors and you notice that another group starts making rivers on the block platform. "What is beneath that contagious, ubiquitous idea?" you might ask. Asking that question may shift your observation lens, and you will become more sensitive to evidence of the big idea behind the children's play. It might be rivers themselves, but it might also be something else entirely. You are now listening for related ideas. Children's associations are not always linear or obvious. At times they are highly symbolic. Your own emotions and imagination can help you realize that an idea has the potential to become something big. You won't know what that something big will be at first, only that it captures the imagination of these particular children.

Interrogate the Topic

Ask yourself if the idea might be significant enough to sustain collaborative research. How do you know an idea is likely to support sustained investigation if the children do engage with it? A compelling idea is necessary, but not sufficient, for sustained research with children. When a promising topic arises, ask, "In my experience, would this topic bear significant research?" Sometimes children are excited about an idea, but you may think that there's not enough there to keep them interested over time. It's a fine distinction, and I suggest that if in doubt, go for it and see what happens. But sometimes it is obvious. For example, I remember one group of children who were fascinated with drawing Pokemon characters for a short while. We observed both contagion and emotion around the endeavor. And the case may be made that the compelling feature of the topic could have been the social connection the children felt around the topic or competence with drawing. But we made the decision to let the topic go and not take it on as an investigation, believing it would not support significant research.

The image of the significance of the work is different from that in schools that use thematic curricula, where the teacher determines the topic, for example, pumpkins at Halloween. In that pedagogical context, a teacher would offer the children many different encounters with pumpkins, looking for ways to present academic tasks in terms of the theme. Perhaps the children in the thematic classroom would find the activities engaging, but it is unlikely "pumpkin" as a topic will bear significant research, and it certainly won't if the "pumpkin unit" is all created in advance by the teacher. I was that teacher in the first years of my career. What I didn't know was that this kind of approach plugs up the pipeline between teachers and children; it does not require negotiation between them to move forward, nor is it particularly responsive to what the children may bring to the work. The study in these projects is often superficial, limited to what the teacher thinks the concepts around the topic should be. But children don't know those "shoulds". Invariably, they go far deeper and find more significant meaning in a topic they have researched than I ever invited them to when I was planning their encounters thematically. The significance of the work in the thematic classroom lies in whether pre-determined understandings are acquired. In contrast, thinking teachers who facilitate children's research consider the significance of the work in terms of the children's sustained engagement, symbolic thinking and representation, and intellectual growth.

All that said, there have been times when I was mistaken about whether a topic would bear significant work. I had always considered pop culture as diminishing for children and did not have Disney anything in the classroom. But one year the children were passionate about the movie "Frozen." I resisted all the signs of a compelling idea. No way could significant work come from a Disney film! But the children were insistent, persistent, and passionate in their Frozen play, conversation, and representation. Finally, I capitulated, and what resulted was a wonderful, surprise, long-term investigation that was not in the least superficial or silly (see Oken-Wright 2014 for more of this story).

The significance of a topic for children's research can grow over time. The following mini-story is the beginning of an investigation that started with a fairly mundane provocation and ended up as a deep and long-term research project into good vs. evil and the children's growing power to vanquish that which frightens them.

A Topic Shifts and the Teacher Shifts with It

One day the children were testing the Lego boats they had made to see if they would float. I observed and thought 'This is about the physics of sinking and floating.' Though the children were enjoying the experiment, I didn't sense that it was a particularly powerful moment. Until, that is, Janelle's boat started to sink. The five-year-old put her hands under the boat and declared it afloat. I invited the children to talk about their experiments with the boats in our next class meeting, as I often did to learn what the children were thinking about what they had done during the morning. Janelle told a version of her experience, saying, 'When I took my hands out, it still floated. It was magical. Maybe that water had magic! Magic is real!' Suddenly the energy of the group exploded. Where the children were merely participating in the conversation about sinking and floating Lego boats, they were passionate about whether magic was real or not. This was not at all where I thought the morning was going, but there was no denying the electricity around the new topic. That very day the children went on a fairy hunt on the playground, documenting as they went. My hypothesis was this might be worth pursuing, though I had no idea where it would lead. Spoiler alert: where it led was somewhere wonderful, not at all about sinking/floating or about whether or not magic was real. In fact, the ensuing long-term investigation landed on the nature of good VS evil and the power of children to vanquish evil. Through it the children grew their personal resources in a truly meaningful way. (for more of this story, see Oken-Wright 2017).

Flow Challenge: The Project Stalls ◆ 139

Following impassioned conversation about possible fairy sitings, the children documenting the fairies they found in the outdoor classroom.

The children set out to keep count of the fairies they saw on the playground. However, believing that she had seen magic out there as well, Casey decided to divide the paper in half so they could document sightings of both fairies and magic.

You might be asking, "Should I Bring a Topic to the Children?" Teachers are vital participants in the learning stories that happen in their classrooms. That participation looks different from any you would see in a traditional school, however. Whereas a teacher who is guided by scripts and manuals is likely to take all the responsibility for presenting topics of study and lessons (often given to her in the way she "gives" topics to children), if a teacher-researcher brings a topic to children, it will be based on their curiosity and hers. Fed by her observation of the children's play, conversation, and representation, she may be curious about topics like the nature of learning, children's perspective or process, or other topics that can further her understanding of how teaching and learning work. The teacher can also bring an idea to the children or notice their engagement in a naturally occurring event like a surprise rainbow or a cultural event experienced by many of the children. When she does this, however, she will take care that it is not her agenda that she is presenting. Rather, she will take a stance of curiosity, wondering what the children are thinking about the event.

Sometimes you will think you are on a particular path in your research with children based on all the above. And then you notice that in children's play or group conversations about their work, the topic keeps traveling to a different idea or aspect of the original idea. The compelling idea can be fluid. It can be a bit like walking on paths in the woods; you start out on the well-traveled path, but soon a secondary path branches off from the one you started on. Perhaps the smaller path, ever winding, finds the original path again a mile further on. Or perhaps it widens and becomes its own main path. The dynamic, meandering, and unpredictable nature of research with children can be one of its joys.

Documentation

Document the children's interactions with the idea. One valuable insight from the educators in Reggio Emilia is that documentation is an essential pedagogical tool for teachers, children, and families. In an environment that invites rich interactions and deep engagement, teachers observe with intention and create traces of the children's processes and thinking. Those traces may be photographs of children at work; the finished work or pieces that represent stages of the work; video of the children's process; audio recordings; and notes and drawings the teacher made while observing. These traces are just the beginning of the documenting process. The teacher studies the collected data and makes hypotheses about the children's intent. She uses the documentation to imagine possibilities. She interprets their meaning. She may offer a provocation based on her hypotheses about that meaning. Again, she documents, this time, the children's response to the provocation. The connection between documentation and teaching/learning is cyclical, one leading to the other and back again, with learning for children and teachers deepening each time around. Documentation is the catalyst for and foundation of curriculum. Quite different from curriculum that is imposed from without, it is dynamic and organic and comes from within the teaching and learning group. When documentation changes what happens in the classroom, when it informs the teaching and the learning, we consider it pedagogical documentation.

Documenting is deep listening, not just to what children say, but to the meaning behind their words and actions. What is the meaning that children are trying to construct in their play, conversation, and representation? This question frames the work of the teacher-researcher.

When documenting children's thinking and process (including our interpretation) is used to support the learning of children, teachers, families, and colleagues, we can consider it "pedagogical." It is the catalyst for and foundation of curriculum. Quite different from curriculum that is imposed from without, it is dynamic and organic and comes from within the teaching and learning group. For example:

- ♦ In creating documentation, the teacher learns about the children and their thinking, allowing her to recognize the meaning behind children's expressions and make decisions about how to support them in constructing and acting on that meaning.
- ♦ Witnessing the teacher document their process and viewing the documentation itself teaches the children about the importance of their endeavors and the

meaning behind them. It's a more powerful gaze than just watching, and children feel it. It also is an invitation to revisit and idea or relaunch the investigation.
- Reading the learning stories within the documentation informs and inspires colleagues and the children's families.

Documentation includes the process of creating it, the teacher's interpretation of the meaning of it, and dissemination to those who might learn from it: children, families, colleagues, etc. Documentation articles may include notebooks that tell the story of an investigation, videos (possibly made accessible with QR codes posted for viewing), blog posts, or panels, for example. How you display and disseminate documentation depends on who the intended audience is and how to communicate with them best. For example, in schools where parents rarely enter the building, digital dissemination of documentation articles may work best, with more tangible forms available within the school for children's viewing. However, where parents or colleagues frequent, panels created toward the end of an investigation and posted on walls may serve everyone best.

When you choose to step into research with children around a compelling topic, you commit to documenting their interaction with the idea. Documenting children's processes allows us to revisit what we have observed. As much as we think we will remember what we've seen and heard during a day, the traces that we have saved by documenting will so often surprise us! In the process of documenting and studying their documentation, teachers learn about the children and their thinking; they learn about themselves; and they learn about learning as they create and study documentation. Children, too, learn from their teachers' documentation efforts. When they witness their teachers documenting their play, conversations, and representation, children learn that the work they are doing has value beyond their process and perspective. When children interact with the documentation itself, they revisit what they have experienced and have access to new perspectives. Documentation is an inextricable part of the learning that goes on in classrooms where it happens.

Flow Challenge: The Project Stalls ◆ 143

Two children revisit a documentation panel of a research project from earlier in the year.

The Process of Documenting

To begin, we observe and listen in a rich and provocative environment, armed with tools to capture moments in time: cameras, voice recorders, video recorders, or smart phones or tablets with those capabilities, as well as notepads and pens. With those tools, we collect traces of children's processes: photographs of them at work, the children's products or images of them, video recordings, audio recordings, notes, and quotes. We transcribe significant conversations. While the experience we are documenting is relatively fresh in mind, we use the raw data we have gathered and create a provisional learning story…a first draft, in a way. My approach was to gather the raw data and create blog posts with narratives and my initial interpretations, which I shared with parents and kept for my research. I printed the blog posts out and displayed them on a clipboard accessible to the children. This made the documentation available for inspiration and revisitation. You may develop a different system, but the basics are the raw data, some sort of narrative, and your interpretation of the children's intent and meaning.

The images, transcriptions of conversations, and notes that make documentation support our memories about the children's process. As the investigation proceeds, we continue to gather and study all of the raw data and our provisional narratives and interpretations. Patterns will emerge, and our understanding of children's meaning will grow, weaving documentation into the fabric of learning and teaching in the classroom.

What Do I Document?

The teacher-researcher makes decisions about what and how to document every day. You might document what appears to be particularly significant to the children, or what the children undertake that is related to your own curiosity about them and their process. You may choose to document one child's process (as in his process of sculpting a figure in clay) or that of a small group. You may choose what to document based on a hunch that there's something more underneath the children's play around a particular topic. You may be curious about the children's response to a particular provocation. Or you may have a particular question that you are interested in researching, so you choose to document whatever goes on in the classroom related to that question.

You cannot document everything that goes on in your classroom. With experience creating and studying documentation, significant ideas will escape your attention less and less often. Meanwhile, try to be intentional about what you choose to document. Think about the process as an investigation; you are searching for children's intent, and when you think you've found it, treat it as provisional, subject to change, for that's what it is. Keep playing. Take raw documentation back to the children and see what happens. Document their response.

Documentation is integral to any research process. Scientists document their own process, and older children can, too. In an early childhood setting, the teacher does most of the data collection, interpreting, and reporting/publishing. Documentation is not separate from the research itself. Rather, there's a sort of cyclical dialogue that occurs between children and teacher-researchers: initial provocation, data gathering, teachers' study of the documentation, teachers' interpretation and hypothesis, provocation, children's response to the provocation, more data gathering and interpretation, and so on.

Interpretation

It is not enough to collect the traces of activity in the classroom. Interpreting the data you collect, finding meaning in the children's play, conversation, and representation, is what makes documenting the powerful pedagogical tool it is. It is likely that your interpretation of a particular research project will go through several iterations. For example, after an interesting encounter in the classroom, your initial notes may lead you to a provisional interpretation. As the project proceeds and you continue to document, new meanings may emerge and your interpretation may become deeper, more nuanced, or more specific. This can happen several times during the course of the project.

Choosing what to document is the very first act of interpretation in the documentation process. If you choose to focus your documenting efforts on a budding research project with children, documenting can help you trace the trajectory it takes. Studying your initial data (photographs, recordings, videos, notes) and articulating an initial interpretation can help you form hypotheses about how to support the children's research. In addition, bringing documentation back to the children allows them to revisit their experiences and their theories, which can help keep the momentum going or help support relaunch.

Your interpretation of documentation and where you imagine the children's research may go will revolve around a number of questions:

- What are the children trying to express, communicate, or figure out? The answer to this question may not be obvious. Children may have explicit intent, that is, intent they express directly, such as "I'm going to paint a house." They may also have implicit intent, a big idea or concept, often much deeper than the explicit intent, that they want to explore or figure out (Oken-Wright & Gravett, 2002). Sometimes the implicit intent emerges deep into the research. But we want to prime ourselves for its existence from the beginning.
- What help can I offer that would support the children's efforts to realize their intent at this moment?
- Where might the children go with this research? (this is to prime your mind for the possibilities) and
- If I have a hypothesis about the big idea behind the children's research, what provocation(s) would support that intent? Think with colleagues if you can: What are all the possibilities? Again, this is mind-priming. Once you have generated a list of possible provocations, do nothing…yet. Patience as you continue to observe the children's process with a new lens allows you to make an informed assessment about what aspect of the topic really speaks to the children.

Provocation and Response

As an invitation to play, explore, and/or represent an idea, the provocation can be an object or event that captures the imagination and piques curiosity. It can be a question, a phenomenon, a problem, or an object. A good classroom environment is a collection of provocations. You might look around and, with a critical eye, see if you can identify existing or naturally occurring "ponder provocations" like effects from a prism in the window, a flower's blooming in progress, the music from metal pots left under dripping eaves in the outdoor classroom, or shadows cast by branches outside a sunny window. A ponder provocation might be naturally occurring or you might bring one and simply place it in the classroom, such as an array of natural materials with magnifying glasses, paper, and pens; windchimes outside the classroom windows; or large squares of multi-colored translucent silk fabric. Think about the things you find wonder-inspiring. That awareness can give you an idea of what a provocation is and what it's for.

Once you have hypothesized that an idea may be compelling for the children, poke it. Identify salient ideas from the children's expressions. Bring those ideas back to them in conversation. Bring images of their work around the idea to your class meeting and see where the dialogue inspired by those images and ideas goes. Inviting children to revisit an experience is a provocation. When you have questions about the children's intent or want to invite the children to delve deeper into their curiosity and interest, you might offer a provocation.

If your observations of children's play, conversations, and representation lead you to think an idea is compelling enough to pursue, offer provocations to test your hypothesis about what is meaningful to the children. When you do, observe their response. What they do with the provocation can prove or disprove your theory about the children's intent. If the provocation is on target, the children are likely to engage with it well, and the provocation will provide an opportunity for them to engage with their research anew. If the provocation falls flat, it's OK. It is information. You now know what the children's intent is not and can observe longer or have more conversations with the children to learn more.

Here is a brief story about a particular naturally-occurring ponder provocation that led to some significant research.

Every year we asked the children to bring boots to leave at school. It was an unusually dry end of summer, and by the end of September we hadn't seen a drop of rain. One day one of the children asked, "Why do we have boots here if it's never going to rain?"

"So when it rains you can go puddle stomping," I replied.

Anticipating puddle stomping created a well of wonder that lasted until the first rain...a drizzly rainfall a few weeks later. Excited to go puddle stomping, the children put on their boots and went outside, but they found not one puddle. This ponder problem started an impassioned attempt by the children first to find puddles somewhere on campus and then, when that failed, to make puddles (it was more difficult than you would think), which led to a research project about the nature of water, the earth that sucked the water in, and, eventually, dams, "oceans," and rivers. All from the ponder problem of boots in the classroom and no rain.

For a provocation to be effective, it should be open-ended (i.e., there is no one correct response) and capture the imagination of the children. Tiny moments of wonder and surprise can become big research projects, but if they don't, they are still valuable in and of themselves. You can't make the big projects happen. Instead, listen to the children and ask questions that keep them wondering. Offer materials when they are needed. Enter the investigation *together* with the children and, as the one with power to do so, let it have a natural lifespan.

Reciprocal Provocations

In the course of any investigation, teachers and children may engage in a sort of ongoing exchange of provocations. The children offer a provocation to the teacher, which inspires his curiosity; after some study of the children's expressions, he offers the children a provocation. The children's response to the provocation is a provocation for the teacher, and so on. Here is an example of the reciprocity between provocations for children and teachers beginning with a windy day.

Provocation for the children:	The wind is howling, and the children hear it.
Provocation for the teacher:	The children comment on the sound they are hearing and identify it as the wind. They engage in a brief conversation among themselves, which the teacher witnesses.
Provocation for the children:	In the class meeting, the teacher reminds the children about their comments about the wind, leaving the door open for a conversation.

Provocation for the teacher: The children express many theories about the wind. The teacher feels their excitement. At one point in the conversation, there is conflict around whether or not you can see the wind and if so, what it looks like.

Provocation for the children: The teacher offers a provocation for those who are interested: Show us what wind might look like. She chooses to offer the Smart Board for this work, to encourage dialogue about the children's theories.

Drawing their ideas on the Smart Board, the children pose theories about what wind might look like if you could see it.

Afterward, the children spontaneously make kites. The teacher invites them to take the kites with them when they go outdoors. The children find many ways to "fly" their kites, indoors and outdoors.

The children found ways to fly their kites in novel ways.

The children's theory was that if we turned on the fan, they would be able to fly their kites indoors. However, this kite flew right onto a friend and stuck there: not what the girls expected!

Provocation for the children: The teacher prints out the Smart Board screen and later, as the children continue to think about wind, she offers new provocations: a resource and a question. The resource is the printout of the children's representations of wind, and the question, derived from one of the several conversations they had about wind, "How could you catch the wind?" The children took the printout to the outdoor classroom and used it to hypothesize together about how to catch the wind so they could see it.

Provocations can be invitations to represent, explore, or act on the questions and topic at hand. As you can see from the story, above, they do not stand alone. Rather, we might consider them a type of dialogue between children and teachers, each acting in response to the other's invitation.

To know if, when, or what to offer as a provocation, listen with curiosity to what children say in small or large group conversations. Do the children have an idea about what they may want to do about the research question? Do ideas emerge that make you wonder about the children's deeper intent? Check in with them to see if your hypothesis resonates with them. Or offer materials or an experience to test your hypothesis. Does a small group want to investigate a particular aspect of the question? Is there a goal that the children want to set for themselves? Consider the example of one long-term investigation about the source and nature of snow a group of five-year-olds engaged in after a rare snowstorm. The provocations for children and their responses (which are provocations for the teacher) are in italics.

- It began with the provocation of a *naturally occurring event* (snowfall after five years of snowless winters).
- *The children showed their interest in conversation and in their bodies*, excited about the first snowfall many had experienced in their lives.

- I offered a provocation: *an invitation to the children in the form of a question/request* ("Tell me about snow").
- We held a *class conversation*.
- The children presented me with a provocation: *"We think that if we learn how to make snow, we will understand how God does it. Let's make snow!"*

After the initial conversations about snow, I hypothesized that the children were interested in both the nature of snowflakes and the source of snow, and thus began a sustained research project and the concomitant exchange: children's expression→teacher's response→children's response and so on, through many iterations, until the children had figured out to their satisfaction how snow is made. To read the whole story "How It Snows," see Oken-Wright (2004, pp. 175–194).

Group Work

Work with small groups to realize their intent. As you meet with small groups, look for opportunities to invite collaboration. Once you have a hypothesis about what the children are trying to figure out and have tested it with one or more provocations, collaborate with the children to determine the action part(s) of the research. From there, a small group may take on the project as a whole or several small groups may take on different aspects of the research challenge. You might solicit volunteers for small groups or invite specific children, depending on your assessment of the learning possibilities. For example, a group may consist of children who share a passion for the topic, or you may invite children who bring different gifts to the project. As with everything the thinking teacher does, you will want to be intentional about group formation and know why you are making the choices you are making.

The dynamics within the small group are a matter of layers of intelligence. That is, the individual brings her intelligence to the group, which nudges everyone's understanding to a new level. In turn, that individual is enriched by the thinking of the others. Each member of the group grows individually and enriches other individuals in the group. In the process, the group as an entity develops its own intelligence, separate from individual growth but very much in the mix. If there are five children in the group, there will be six intelligences, all affecting each other: five children and the sixth entity, the group itself.

Though you may have ideas about how you think the project will go, it is important not to make that happen. Rather, you will want to take an improvisational stance, thinking "Yes and..." to the children's proposals. How the research goes is negotiated among the children and with you. Keep in mind that your primary role is to help the children realize their intent, which may or may not be explicit. You often have to work a bit to learn what is really underneath the children's passion for a topic.

The Reciprocity between Small Group and Whole Group

Bring the small groups' progress back to the whole group periodically. As a small group works on their research, invite them to apprise the rest of the class of their progress every now and again. Sometimes, this is just informative, but small groups may also go to the whole group to ask for help thinking about a problem within the research (see Chapter 14). Create a system so that the children realize that this is an option when they are stuck. For example, you may want to set aside some meeting time for small group to whole group communication. When there is an exchange of ideas back and forth, small group to whole group, the flow of inspiration can keep a research project alive. Chapter 11 tells the story of the Cardinal investigation, a research project in which the children set out to lure cardinals to our new front yard. The children thought of several ways to test their hypotheses and several ideas for realizing their goals. It wouldn't have been possible to execute all the ideas at once, so some of the plans sat on the shelf for a while. For example, the first idea, to make a hiding tree so that the children could observe the bird feeder unseen, was large enough that, over the many days of the tree's construction, some children left the group and others joined. Because the progress of the project was made public on a regular basis, the flow into and out of the groups could be fluid.

Everyone knew and was interested in what was going on with the small groups. When it was time to take on another of the planned sub-projects within the Cardinal investigation, the children were able to make informed choices about joining a new small group. That small group, too, kept the rest of the class apprised of their progress, which inspired even more ideas for relaunching the project. When the children completed all the original sub-projects, they showed us that they were not ready to abandon the topic. They themselves created other sub-projects. Those small groups also reported on their progress periodically in our class meetings. Even though every child may not participate in a small group, the flow of information from small group to whole group lets a project like this belong to everyone. Direct invitations from small group members to the rest of the class keep everyone in the loop, as do teachers' documentation and children's representations.

Relaunch

Be aware of opportunities to "relaunch" an investigation. Relaunch of an investigation may happen when there is a renewal of interest in a project after an accidental or intentional interruption. Or it could be that the children planned multiple sub-projects, and they relaunch the investigation when they are ready to take on a new one. Whatever its purpose, the relaunch is part of the sustainability of long-term research. Children's research may be relaunched if it has stalled because of sticking points, children's interest shifts to a new aspect of the original idea, or an interruption occurs in the school calendar. The thinking teacher uses these opportunities to relaunch as chances to renew the energy and investment in a research project.

How do you support the relaunch of a research project? You might bring documentation of the project to a meeting to remind the children of their participation in the research. That might be enough to start the process of relaunch. If not, just ask the children what they'd like to do about the topic. It is always possible that the children's interest has waned, in which case relaunch may not be appropriate. But they may just as well want to continue or to investigate some other aspect of the idea or even be inspired by what they have already done to investigate something else entirely. You can see how important your listening is to this process, as is your openness to the children's expressed and implicit intent (Oken-Wright & Gravett, 2002).

The teacher may be the one to initiate a relaunch. But when children have been engaged deeply with a topic, they may be reluctant to let it go, and they often relaunch the project themselves. In the Cardinal story below, as they were completing planned pieces of the investigation, the children came up with new avenues for investigating the big idea of "luring" and caring for the birds. Living within the research question keeps it alive. And when the research has brought the children pleasure, they tend to want to keep it going.

The Investigation Protocol.

Research with children is alive and unpredictable, and as rewarding and rich as collaborative research with children can be, it can also be susceptible to points of conflict along the way. Those sticking points...sometimes uncomfortable and often a point of inner conflict for the teacher...can derail a promising investigation if the teacher doesn't have a way to address them. The Investigation Protocol can help the teacher-researcher appreciate the moving parts of supporting children's research. It can help you get started. And it can help turn potential points of conflict into opportunities.

References

Oken-Wright, P. (2004). "Embracing Snow: A Story of Negotiated Learning" in Hendrick, J., ed. *Next Steps Toward Teaching the Reggio Way: Accepting the Challenge to Change.* Pearson. 175–194.

Oken-Wright, P. (2014). *Project Frozen: An Unexpected Investigation.* eBook at pokenwright.com.

Oken-Wright, P. (2017). *The Evolution of Courage: The Power of Imagination and Intellect to Conquer Fear.* eBook at pokenwright.com.

Oken-Wright, P. & Gravett, M. (2002). "Big Ideas and the Essence of Intent" in Fu, H., ed. *Teaching and Learning: Collaborative Exploration of the Reggio Emilia Approach.* Merrill Prentice Hall. 197–220.

11

The Cardinal Story

In a meeting conversation like many others, a child recalled having seen a cardinal at her house. What followed was one of those awe-inspiring moments for me. The perfectly matter-of-fact observation from one child sparked great interest in the assembled group. All the children shared a desire to lure cardinals to the schoolyard, which they could see through the expanse of windows in the classroom. They did not agree on whether they should try to catch the birds. But they were all eager to see a cardinal. This is the story of how one child's observation initiated an impassioned and sustained investigation.

For days after the initial conversation, the children engaged in dialogue to plan and negotiate several sub-projects, with a shared purpose of letting the children see – and maybe capture – a cardinal (the recognition of a compelling idea). The children knew that installing feeders might lure the birds to them, so that is where they began. They continued to talk. Consensus as to how to proceed ended there. Some children wanted to catch a cardinal; some did not.

Do We Want to Catch the Cardinals?

Isabella: No. 'Cause they might get hurt.
Georgia: Cause then they might die, and we won't have a lot of Virginia state birds.

DOI: 10.4324/9781003625568-14

Peyton: And they're fragile.
Sienna: And if they die a lot, we won't have any of them.

The Children Take the Perspective of the Birds

Teacher: What if we do see them?
Regan: Let them eat the food and say, "Birdie, birdie, come eat your food."
Evans: But they don't understand our voices.
Georgia: Also, birds are afraid of us, so we should be hiding so we can see them without them seeing us.
Evans: But there aren't a lot of trees!

Proposing to Hide Behind a Tree

Maggie: Well, we could make a nest out of paper, and then we could put it in a tree. And we can make a home for the birds with leaves in it.
Georgia: Birds don't like the scent of humans, so they won't live there. Because they're scared of us.
Maggie: We could plant a tree [to hide behind], but that could take a really long time.
Adelaide: You only have to find an acorn and throw it in the dirt.
Teacher: How long does it take a tree to grow?
Bella: A thousand days.
Maggie: What about fifteen hours or something?
Teacher: Do you want to wait that long before you hide?
Children: No!

To Disguise as a Cardinal ... or Not

Evans: I have a great idea. What if we made cardinal costumes and then maybe they will come?
Several voices: Yeah!
Honor: That's so they'll think we're real cardinals.

Evans: How about we wear the cardinal costumes any day we want the cardinals to come?!

Hartley: I don't think the birds will think we're real cardinals when we wear the costumes. Because they might think we're cardinal giants, and they might run away from us.

Luring Cardinals with Images of Other Cardinals

Isabella: We could make a bird, and then we could put it somewhere, and then a cardinal will think that it's a real cardinal.

Teacher: Will the cardinal think it's a good place to come, then?

Children: Yes.

Bella: We would draw a cardinal and draw a cardinal on a rock.

Georgia: I think we should make a giant cardboard cardinal. We should make it poking their beak in the water so they will come. No, maybe just a small one.

Adelaide: Yeah, they would be scared, and they would fly away.

Some of the children had experience with cardboard in water, and they convinced the others that cardboard was not a good medium for making cardinals that would lure other cardinals. But rocks were still on the table.

The children generated all these ideas in a series of community conversations. After each one, they spontaneously represented cardinals and began to spread the word to children in the other class in the building. The energy, passion, and contagion around this idea told us that somewhere in this topic was a compelling idea, one that would support sustained engagement. Was it really about cardinals? Or birds in general? I had done enough action research around the big ideas that engage the imaginations of children (and, often, adults) transcending time, geography, and cultural differences to know that an idea this compelling probably had something deeper behind it. With a provisional theory in mind, we took the project on.

Of all the ideas the children generated, the "hiding tree" garnered the most attention, so the children and teachers chose that as a starting place, with the promise that the adults would remind the children of their other ideas later. Since they knew that growing a tree would take too long, the children proposed to make one. To begin to develop a shared image of the hiding tree, we took a small group of children to a suitable tree on campus with clipboards and pens and invited them to study the tree through drawing. Doing such a study does more than inform children about the nature of a tree. It also helps to construct a group identity around the project, bringing minds together, in a way.

With the knowledge about the nature of trees they constructed through drawing, the children articulated their intentions for the tree: life-sized, big enough to hide behind. We offered them pool noodles to serve as an armature. Working in a small group, the children taped the noodles together and covered the whole structure with papier mâché, which they made with some assistance. The process took a few days, during which group membership was fluid.

Though the project was initiated by one class, interest was high among all the children in the building, and soon everyone in both classes was engaged. When one group had a conversation that pertained to the investigation, members of that group shared their ideas with the other class in their meetings. Similarly, when a phase

Tree studies.

The Cardinal Story ◆ 161

Pool noodles served as an armature for a tree "big enough to hide us."

Papier Mache goes onto the armature.

of construction began or was finished, the small groups were eager to share their progress with their own class and with the other.

Once the trunk was constructed, the children declared, "We need branches!"

"How do you want to make the branches?" I asked, thinking the children might continue the construction methods they'd been using. But they replied, "With sticks from real trees."

So, we took a stick-collecting walk, and the children chose the fallen branches they thought would serve the purpose. Ruminating on the bark on the branches, the children declared that to make the tree trunk seem "real," they would need to paint it a true tree color. They used a stick from a real tree as a referent in order to create the exact color paint they were looking for.

Children paint the trunk with a color they mixed themselves to match the branches.

The children test the hiding tree's effectiveness. "Can we watch the birds without being seen?" they wonder.

I thought perhaps this phase of the project was finished when the children declared the tree's hiding potential satisfactory. But they were not finished. Though this part of the project occurred in January, when many of our trees were bare, the children's assessment of the hiding tree was that it needed leaves, and that they should be green. A new small group was formed to study leaves and construct them from Model Magic.

Throughout the investigation, the teachers acted as memory proxies. When the hiding tree was finished, we held a meeting to remind the children about the plans they had made earlier and to gauge the group's intention. The children relaunched the project with the plan to paint cardinals on rocks, which they figured

The finished hiding tree

would attract live cardinals to the feeders. At this point in the year, the children had adopted the Study Protocol (Chapter 13) as their own, and they asked for images of cardinals to use as referents. We collaborated with the children to find the "right" images for the class tablets, and the children used them as referents as they studied the birds. Their goal: paint cardinals that looked enough like real cardinals to attract the birds to the feeders.

A study of the documentation we'd created at this point led us to a provisional theory that the big idea behind the children's passion in the project was making the invisible visible, a challenge I knew from experience children find compelling (Oken-Wright & Gravett, 2002). In fact, you will see evidence

The Cardinal Story ◆ 165

The children researched and studied cardinals through drawing in preparation for painting them on rocks.

A child uses her cardinal study as a referent to draw the image on a piece of slate the children and teachers agreed would serve as a rock.

The painted cardinal rocks placed near the bird feeder to attract real cardinals to the feeder.

of this commonality in other stories in this book, for example, the "Layers of Attraction" project in Chapter 12, in which a group of children set out to lure a chipmunk out of hiding. Understanding the allure of big ideas gives a thinking teacher one perspective when trying to determine whether an idea is compelling enough to support sustained inquiry. It also led us to suspect that the children's passion about cardinals was not, actually, about the birds themselves. I would caution that knowing that an idea is a universal question does not give us license to make lists of big ideas to take to children. Rather, it is one clue as to the meaning children are constructing about a topic. In the cardinal investigation, understanding big ideas did not lead us to an immediate interpretation, but a provisional one, as if to say to ourselves, "What if this is what the children are trying to understand?"

Cardinals did, indeed, visit the feeders, inspiring great excitement and adding to the sustainability of the investigation. I have noticed that in children's research, there exists a certain reciprocity between intellect and emotion/imagination that fosters both. In this case, excitement over success with the painted rocks relaunched the investigation yet again. In this iteration, the children made a plan to lure more birds to the feeders with their own bodies, dressed up like cardinals (and a rock) so as not to frighten the birds.

The children, costumed and hiding behind the hiding tree lest they frighten the birds away, continued to watch the birds

The Cardinal Story ◆ 167

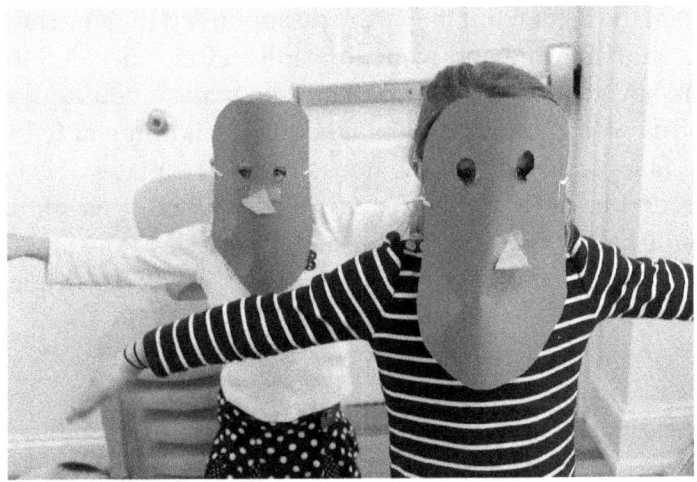

Cardinals, ready to fool the real cardinals so that, when they come to the feeder, they will not be afraid of the bird watchers.

This child is disguising herself as a rock. The children considered their success in luring cardinals to the feeder with the painted rocks proof that cardinals are not afraid of rocks.

frequent the feeder. But they were disappointed that the cardinals at the feeders came and went so readily. Honor decided to take action. She proposed that if the children made a house for them, the birds would be right there when the children wanted to see them. She proposed that the house should be made of clay and proceeded to draw a plan for the house. When it was finished, Honor asked to present her idea at our next class meeting.

The children liked Honor's plan and considered adding to it.

Peyton suggested, 'What if we made the birds some clothes?'

Honor: But how could we put them on without scaring them?
Evans: I have a idea. What if we put them in the bird house? THEN they put them on theirselves.
Honor: The birds don't get to decide. If the birds decide whether to put clothes on, what if they never put them on and they slip and get broken?
Teacher: Because you know that cloth on the floor is dangerous? (Yes)
Georgia: I have an idea. Maybe we could make the birds really hungry and then when he's eating, we could put on the clothes.
Honor: But he might see us and fly away from eating the bird seed.
Georgia: But what if he's really hungry and he doesn't want to fly away?
Honor: Well, usually he does, because birds don't want to be trapped even more than they don't like being hungry. So if they're really hungry they still will fly away.
Peyton: What are the birds going to sleep on?
Honor: We could work on making a bed in the house.
Maggie: Maybe we could make it out of hay.

Honor's plan to make a birdhouse became everyone's plan, including with children in the other class. Together, the children continued to hypothesize about the best medium for the job, eventually settling on clay through some impressive logical thinking. In this way, the shared purpose of the Cardinal Project

The children worked collaboratively to construct a birdhouse according to Honor's plan.

evolved from luring cardinals forth to inspiring them to stay, yet another relaunch initiated by the children.

When others began to lose interest in the project, Honor was reluctant to let it go. The investigation protocol is flexible enough that individuals can continue with the research whether others

Painting the birdhouse.

are still engaged or not. In this case, witnessing the process of an individual investigation inspired the other children to revisit the research. The pleasure Honor found in collaboration led her to share the plan, and the birdhouse became a small group project.

When children engage in purposeful, collaborative, and sustained investigation, they often play and represent the topic spontaneously again and again, in different ways. For quite some time after the birdhouse iteration, the children continued to study and represent cardinals. One child initiated a project to document the birds that visit the feeders with photos and text. At one point, a group of children declared intent to create a play about the cardinals. With the help of their teacher, who acted as a scribe and cleared a path for production, they wrote and produced a play about birds who were actually the children themselves, enchanted. They "published" their work by performing the play for the other class. The children continued to watch for cardinals (and extrapolate to other birds) not only around the birdhouse and feeder, but all around them at school and at home, and chose to represent cardinals in multiple languages for some time going forward.

The Cardinal project left the children in both classes with such a sense of agency and power to make a difference in their world! They formulated a question (How can we lure the cardinals

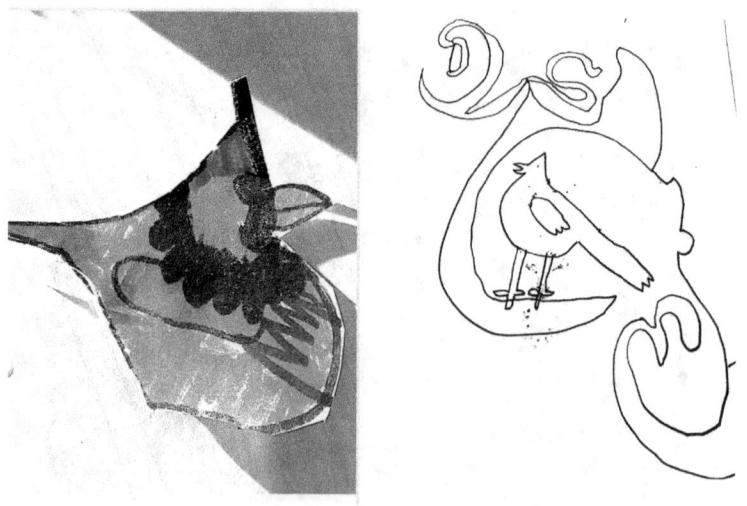

Parallel to the group's research, the children spontaneously studied the nature of cardinals through multiple languages.

to us so we can study them?), researched the topic (studying through drawing in the context of the project and also on their own), had many class conversations to co-construct theory about cardinals and to formulate plans to answer their questions, acted on their theories, worked collaboratively in fluid small groups, represented their ideas in multiple media, shared their findings with their own class and with the other class, and relaunched the research multiple times. Using the Investigation Protocol helped keep all the adults involved (two teachers and two assistant teachers) on the same page, guided our documentation throughout, provided for collaborative study of the documentation and the plan for provocations, and helped us stay awake to the children's efforts to relaunch.

Consider This

- The Cardinal Story is brought to you by documentation. Without it, the story and the learning opportunity for us as educators would have been lost. Where in the story can you find the other elements of the Investigation Protocol? What is the relationship between the elements? For example, how does each depend on and enhance the others?
- Create an itinerary of a project from your research with children. Include all the provocations that occurred for the children and you. What can you learn when you see the itinerary in this form?
- Are there elements of the Investigation Protocol that you imagine you could have used to sustain children's research where it faltered? What would you like to try next?

Reference

Oken-Wright, P. & Gravett, M. (2002). "Big Ideas and the Essence of Intent" in Fu, H., ed. *Teaching and Learning: Collaborative Exploration of the Reggio Emilia Approach*. Merrill Prentice Hall. 197–220.

12

Points of Conflict in Children's Research

A project may stall for a number of reasons, and you may feel stuck. Sometimes, when no significant research has occurred, you may be worried that it never will. As rewarding as engaging with children and their research is, you will be faced with sticking points unique to this way of teaching. Uncertainty, mismatches between children's intent, which they have come to expect to realize, and their ability, and cognitive conflict among children are examples of conflict that arises *because* of the deep and rich engagement children and teachers experience. When the thinking teacher has an idea about why a project is stalling, or why no investigation is emerging at all, he can call on flexible protocols to guide him. The following are some of the situations teachers have told me hamper their attempts to support children's research and a story that illustrates flexible protocols that can help.

Point of Conflict

I have an environment that meets all the criteria for deep engagement, but no research project has emerged.

The children's play, conversation, and representation in your rich environment offer you a window into their thinking and imagination, and you are documenting their process. What do you do now?

Your initial interaction with a group of children after you have an inkling that an idea has caught their imagination may be as simple as asking, "Tell me about _____." Not "what you know about" or "what you wonder about," just "about." That leaves the door open for children to articulate what they are thinking whether it's something they know or wonder or not. Don't be too quick to jump to action. Give yourself time to learn as much as you can about what children's interest is telling you in those first conversations and from children's play and representation following those conversations. Sometimes, what you see in children's play is not what you think it is. Taking a listening stance. Ask clarifying questions. Document and study that documentation. Holding your hypotheses about the children's intent for a bit before acting will allow you to stay open to what else the children have to say. This is how we learned to look beyond the birds for meaning in the Cardinal Story in Chapter 11. Look for a balance between listening and speaking that allows you to be a facilitator and a guide while searching for the deeper meaning of the children's expressions.

The Investigation Protocol guides you toward your next steps. You are embarking upon a recursive process of observe/document → study/hypothesize → invite → observe/document and so on. It's a vertical helix of sorts, with the children's understanding and your insight growing steadily as you ride the helix. The Cardinal Story illustrated the process: a group of children picked up on one small comment with enthusiasm and cognitive conflict, which alerted the teacher to the possibility of something bigger. Other conversations followed, in which the children made plans. And then they were off and running.

Point of Conflict

Every time I think we might be launching an investigation, nothing comes of it.

Ask yourself why.

Could it be that the topic is not compelling enough for the children that it will support sustained investigation?

Are you inadvertently interfering with the children's agency around the topic?

Are you assuming you already know what the big idea is? It may not be apparent until late in the research. The thinking teacher *discovers* the children's deeper intent; she does not create it.

Do the children have the skills this research would require? If not, and the idea is a compelling one, they might develop those skills by engaging with the topic with a little extra support with tools and techniques from you.

The following research project happened so early in the school year that the children did not yet have many of the skills they would have used to realize their intent had the investigation happened later in the year. As you read, you will see that, with a bit more support to collaborate, have good conversations, and represent their ideas in multiple languages and dimensions, the children not only satisfied their curiosity but also developed a disposition to collaborate, conversational skills, and competence in multiple languages.

Layers of Attraction

> At carpool on a day in the second week of school, five-year-old Molly, some friends, and my assistant teacher observed a chipmunk scamper across the yard and then perch up on a piece of slate leaning against a rock for a few minutes before it 'scurried' (Molly's word) away. As they watched the chipmunk the children and the teacher held a running conversation about it. I joined the group in time to hear the assistant teacher say that she had seen that chipmunk in the yard before. Molly must have been skeptical, because she proposed, 'We can paint a stripe on the chipmunk's tummy to see if he comes back and back. But how are we gonna put it on him? Sounds like a mystery to solve.'
>
> Brook observed, 'It's like Scooby Doo. We might have to get a professional for that!'

Hoping to keep the conversation going, I asked, 'How will you catch him to paint a stripe on him?'

Molly proposed, 'We can make a trap! We should put some acorns inside the cage. And make a drawbridge with a string. If you pull the string, the drawbridge goes up. We have to keep him in the cage. We have to put something sticky on the cage, so he'll stick there while we paint the stripe.'

The energy and excitement about Molly's idea prompted me to ask the children if they would like to take the idea to the whole class. They said yes, but while they were waiting for the meeting where that would happen, some of the children drew their image of such a trap.

The spontaneous representation and planning was affirmation that this idea had captured the children's imaginations well enough to make it worth bringing to the whole class to see if there might be broader interest in the idea.

One of the children who first observed the chipmunk draws a plan for a trap to catch the chipmunk.

Note that these young five-year-olds (some still on the cusp of 4) had known each other only a few days. Having come from no preschool or a traditional preschool experience, they had little familiarity with many of the materials they would use as languages later in the year, and their understanding of group meetings was that the teacher talked, and they listened, or she asked questions, and they answered them. How, I wondered, would embarking on what could be a significant project work? That was my research question. How to find out if it was the same chipmunk that came 'back and back' was the children's research question. I decided to go for it.

I invited the children who had engaged in the initial conversation and who had already drawn plans for the trap to bring their ideas to our class meeting. My hypothesis was borne out: if I invited the original posers of the question to make it public, the other children would become engaged. It might not have been, in which case I would have used the idea's failure to catch on as information: what does this tell me about this idea with these children at this time?

Here are some excerpts from that first conversation as the children responded to the provisional plans the original small group presented.

Mariah: What if the chipmunk doesn't know how to read BUT we could hide behind the (shade) umbrella and read the signs and he [will] know what to do, and then he walks in…

Molly: I have some good news. What if we speak to the chipmunk and show him the way to the chipmunk trap? (demonstrating moving like a chipmunk)

Georgia: How do we speak chipmunk?

Teacher: What is chipmunk language? Do you have to move like that to speak chipmunk language, or can you do it with just with a sound?

Molly:	You have to move to show him [how to] get there.

(The children began to crawl on the floor making chipmunk noises)

Teacher:	Let's think about this for a minute. What do you think the chipmunk would do if he started to come in the yard, and then you started to crawl around in the yard acting like a chipmunk?
Peyton:	Well, then he might run away because we might scare him.
Teacher:	How big is a chipmunk? How big are you?

The children demonstrate.

Teacher:	Hmmm…you are a giant to a chipmunk, aren't you?
Piper:	What about he runs away, scared we might step on him with our foot?
Brook:	But wait a second! He might think we're a chipmunk of the chipmunk giants.
Teacher:	Do you want him to think that we're chipmunk giants?
Children:	Yes! No!
Teacher:	So what will you do?
Brook:	We would have to get a net so we could get him?
Georgia:	No. The chipmunk trap is like the net.
Teacher:	But if we want the chipmunk to think that we're chipmunks…
Brook:	We would have to dress up as a chipmunk?
Teacher:	How would you do that?
Ella:	We could go to the store…
Georgia:	That would be a lot of money for 9 chipmunks!
Teacher:	It would. But in JK you can make anything. (This is a new concept to the children: feel

	free to imagine, because chances are good that we can make it happen) So what could you make to look like a chipmunk?
Molly:	Make a mask!!!
Brook:	If we could just speak in chipmunk we could just bend down, and he would think we were his mom. 'Cause his mom is bigger than him.
Molly:	Then we carry him into the trap, and we pull the string really quick.
Teacher:	We put him in the trap because he came to us because we look like his mom? Is that right?

Here I was articulating my understanding of what the children said, both to check in with the speaker and to help the other children tune into what was said by repeating it. The repetition lends importance to the idea and its child and gives the listeners a second chance to hear it.

Georgia:	But he might bite us if we carry him to the trap.
Brook:	He might think we were gonna put a fire [in the trap].

Translation: We are dangerous

Peyton:	We are giants to the chipmunks.
Georgia:	I'm still not going to hold that chipmunk. At all.
Several Voices:	Me either. I am.
Georgia:	I'm going to paint the stripe.
Brook:	I'm going to hold him.
Teacher:	So are you going to make yourselves look like chipmunks? And we need to learn how to speak chipmunk?
Children:	Yes!
Brook:	I know. We can put a snake right behind him and that will zoom him into the trap?

This group of five-year-olds was quite good at the talking part of having conversations already. I didn't have to work hard to keep the conversation going in that respect.

But the children did need some support to listen to each other, which a transcript doesn't really show. Sometimes I repeated or paraphrased what the speaker said. But I also used body language to draw attention to a speaker with my hand or eyes or with some other praxis.

A multi-week investigation developed from these conversations. We teachers acted as memory proxy, reminding the children what they had proposed earlier at appropriate points. The children experienced so much pleasure when thinking together about the trap and constructing it that they expanded the plan repeatedly. A small group made the trap; other children made clay chipmunks to add to the trap so the living chipmunk would think it's a popular chipmunk hangout; another small group made signs to invite the chipmunks in (including a trick sign: 'A lovely lunch for a girl chipmunk'); some of the children were concerned that the sun might repel the chipmunk, so they made an umbrella/tree with leaves for shade. Once it was all installed in the yard, the children considered how they could observe the trap without scaring the chipmunk away. They disguised themselves as large chipmunks, putting aside earlier concerns that giant chipmunks would scare the little one.

Although all the ideas in this investigation were the children's, this project required more from the teachers than it would have if the children had had more experience with conversation, collaboration, negotiation, and representation in multiple languages. We had a bigger role in keeping conversations going than we would have later in the year. When the children were working with unfamiliar media we offered them tools and lent them techniques in a way that we might not have had to if the investigation had occurred a few months later. We had to stay conscious of offering only the support the children needed to realize their intent and not more. We also periodically reminded children of their declared intent throughout the project and invited small groups to make their work public in class meetings.

The children install the trap door of the chipmunk trap.

One of several clay chipmunks the children made to lure the chipmunks to the trap.

Points of Conflict in Children's Research ♦ 181

A LOVELY LUNCH WITH A GIRL CHIPMUNK

The children made signs for the chipmunks like "Come to this house" and, in a bit of trickery, "A lovely lunch with a girl chipmunk."

The children made masks so that the chipmunk would not recognize them as human and be frightened away.

Installing the trap with all its components: the trap itself, signs, a shade tree, clay chipmunks, and food.

There is always a reason that an investigation, once started, stalls. It is the thinking teacher's "Why" that points to the action she can take or the lesson she can learn from the experience. The process is decision-heavy and sometimes full of uncertainty, but the results are oh-so rewarding.

Consider This

- ♦ What points of conflict have you encountered in supporting children's research? How could the elements of the Investigation Protocol have helped you?
- ♦ Create a physical or virtual comment board and carry a pen and a notepad around with you. Be a fly on the wall and write down comments children make that you find intriguing or that pique your curiosity. Post them to the board and revisit them frequently. What can you learn about the children and their thinking from the comment board? What patterns appear?

13

Flow Challenge

Points of Conflict in Representation

Representation plays a role in all learning. When we represent an idea or object, when we re-create it mentally or physically, we construct understanding. Adults do this by expressing their impressions and making sense of new information through talking, writing, drawing, or even just thinking. We solve problems using the same modalities. How often have you found yourself talking to yourself to work out a problem? Or turning to paper and pen in order to figure something out? The information is transformed, and the problem is solved through the act of representing. Though children may not be able to represent abstractly or through reading or writing, they are quite capable of representing even the most complex ideas through graphic and temporal media, such as drawing, painting, sculpting, constructing, moving, role-playing, etc. When those materials are used to express, communicate, and figure things out, we consider them languages. "The 100 languages of children" is a metaphor educators in Reggio Emilia use to refer to children's many ways of knowing and learning. It is in dialogue with the hundred languages that children represent their biggest ideas. To represent is to learn, and children do it with their bodies and voices with the support of materials and the environment.

Every time a child represents an idea, her understanding of the idea deepens. Every time she represents the idea with a different set of materials, her understanding broadens. For example, sculpting a duck in clay requires a skill set and understanding different from what drawing a duck requires. Try it. Draw a duck. Then, sculpt one in clay. Notice what you have to consider in order to sculpt the duck. Will you think about the duck's legs and feet the same way you did when you drew it? In the process of representing that duck, you will learn more about the duck, the materials, physics (possibly, if the duck is to stand), and, most likely, yourself. Knowing the power of representation in this way, we often invite children to represent a significant idea many times and with many different materials.

Among the symbolic languages children use to represent their thinking are paint, ink, clay, wire, pastels, chalk, and all kinds of paper; music, movement, and drama; loose parts for ephemeral representation and tinkering, and so on.

Because it is the dialogue between child and material that matters, anything can become a language for expression, communication, and/or figuring things out. Even a pile of paper clips or a bunch of sticks found on a nature walk can be a language if it is used as such. Though children derive great pleasure from representing their ideas, it is important not to impose requirements to "make something" with materials too soon. If you allow time for exploring media, the children will show you they are interested in and ready to represent in their own time. There is a natural progression from exploration to representation, and it is not necessarily linear. When children in my class engaged with materials but didn't say that they had an agenda, I encouraged them to recognize and articulate their intent: Did they have a plan to make something? Were they drawing/painting, etc. "stream of consciousness?" Were they exploring the medium? Any of those purposes can be important work. It can all support engagement, and we must honor that.

Using multiple languages to represent one's thinking is not a fringe activity; it is central to children's meaning-making and their learning. So, we invite them into dialogue with materials from a very young age. Of course, the youngest children do not use materials to represent their ideas. When children first encounter materials in the infant-toddler centers, they investigate them playfully. This exploration is necessary if children are to use the materials to represent their ideas. They explore to learn what the materials will do and what they will let them do, to learn the "affordances" of the materials (Forman, 1994). In an interview with Lella Gandini (2005), Giovanni Piazza, atelierista at La Villetta School in Reggio Emilia, says:

> A first encounter for children with materials to explore and act on them is a necessary step in the children's process of knowing. Through such encounters and explorations, children build an awareness of what can happen with materials, and adults build the ability to observe and support the significance of each particular experience.

Even much older children need to explore a medium's affordances before using it to express their ideas or figure something out with it. Have you ever witnessed school-age children messing about with materials they had never seen before when they were expected them to use them for an academic task? They were telling you that you skipped a step in your mind. Exploring affordances is a necessary process.

Responding to the power of dialogue with materials, each school in Reggio Emilia has at least one atelier (studio), in which children use materials to make their thinking visible. Many classrooms also have their own mini ateliers. The work in the studio and the work in the classroom tend to intersect, all in support of the children's research. Each school also has at least one atelierista (studio teacher) who supports not only the children's process but also the teachers' competence and confidence in using materials with the children. In addition, a "studio mentality," an extrapolation from the kind of thinking that goes on in the atelier, is carried to every space in the school. Carlina Rinaldi quotes E. Borghi, who said, "Considering the atelier as a metaphor, I like to say (and I am not the only one) that the whole school has to be a large atelier, where children and adults find their voices in a school that is transformed into a great laboratory of research and reflection" (2005).

Eventually, children use materials and media to represent their imaginations and understandings, their plans and ideas, and whatever they are thinking or feeling. When children have intent to represent but struggle to do so, pedagogical flow is affected. This chapter addresses various sticking points that may emerge as children represent their ideas and the flexible protocols that may address them.

Sticking Point:
The children don't have a shared vision of what they want to represent collaboratively.

If children wish to collaborate to make one representation...a tree for a fairy garden that they are making, for example...they need to have a shared image of that tree. Otherwise, collaboration becomes difficult and engagement elusive if one child imagines a tree like a lollipop, one imagines a tree with branches, and one imagines a Christmas tree. The children may be able to negotiate that shared vision without support. But if not, and if you are wondering how to help, the Shared Idea Protocol can be a helpful guide.

The Shared Idea Protocol

Realizing the necessity of the shared vision, I might use this protocol pre-emptively, before a problem arises. When a group of children articulate an intention to represent something together:

- ♦ Invite the children to a meeting to talk about their plans with each other. Encourage them to articulate and name their vision. They might say, for example, "Tree for the fairy garden," "Out of clay, because we want it to live outside," and "We want it to be bigger than the fairies, because trees are bigger than people."
- ♦ Invite the children to draw their individual ideas of what this tree will look like. This will help them clarify their vision and will be something visible to bring to the group. I found that providing what we called "thinking pens" (black felt tips) for this kind of drawing helpful, as they help children consider form, which is what they need for this process.

- Meet with the children around the drawings. Encourage them to talk about the drawings and perhaps choose one to be a referent for the project. Or the children may choose to create an entirely new plan using elements of multiple drawings. The point here is that the children will have made their thinking visible. Their drawings can help them articulate their ideas to each other. They have a visual referent upon which to base their planning of the tree.
- Facilitate flexibly. You are there not to make decisions about how this will go, but to support the children to create a shared image. Remember, our role as teachers is to help the children realize their intent. Creating the shared image is in service to the children's intent, so we want to keep that intent in mind while allowing it to morph in the process if that's where the children want to take it. We want to encourage children to think beyond ownership of their own drawings or alliances for the sake of the project. I often find that, at first, children tend to "like" their own drawing or that of a particular friend. If

Children who have an idea to create one castle collaboratively meet around the plans they have drawn as proposals for how the castle should look.

you ask the question, "Which drawing (or element of a drawing) gives you the most information about how to make the [tree] do you think?" the children's perspective may shift away from personal ownership. This represents the perspective-taking that collaborative work requires: "My idea is richer because of your idea. And our idea is the richest of all."

Sticking Point:
Children get stuck when trying to make an idea visible
Isabelle wanted to paint a horse lying down. She was confident enough to make this plan, but as she began to paint, she did not like the shape or size of the horse's head. She walked away from the easel. Her teacher noticed and invited Isabelle back to the easel to talk about what was happening.

Marcus and Leo declared intent to draw Marcus' new bike from memory. Collaborative drawing can be particularly challenging and quite rich. But at the moment, the boys cannot agree on how the seat should be attached to the bike.

Their teacher might choose to introduce the following protocols to help Isabelle, Marcus, and Leo get unstuck.

The Shared Drawing Protocol

The Shared Drawing protocol can be useful for addressing multiple sticking points in representation, including as support for small groups as they develop a shared idea.

The protocol is an adaptation of Reggie Routman's Shared Writing protocol for early literacy (1991). When you first introduce Shared Drawing, the children direct the teacher as she draws the subject of the investigation. This can take place with a small group or with the whole class, depending on the situation. It helps to do shared drawing on a vertical surface for visibility and to use a whiteboard so that the inevitable "mistakes" the teacher makes can be corrected easily. The teacher draws whatever the children direct her to draw, exactly as they instruct. She makes no assumptions as to their meaning. So, if a child says,

The children direct the teacher's pen in this Shared Drawing session.

"Draw a circle," the teacher draws a circle of any size at any spot on the whiteboard. It is likely that she will guess wrong according to the children's intent. They may cry, "Noooo!" and realize that they must give the teacher more specific instructions. Being entirely responsive to the children's direction, the teacher is helping the children articulate their ideas more completely, listen to each other, and experience the usefulness of the protocol for their own purposes. She is also demonstrating the process of getting one's ideas from the mind to the paper. Once children have a disposition toward collaboration and an understanding of Shared Drawing, they can not only give direction but also share the pen.

 I have found that, in time, the children adopt the Shared Drawing protocol for themselves, and I am no longer needed. The children come to understand the need for a shared image and use the protocol spontaneously and collaboratively.

Sometimes, children's lack of experience and/or confidence in representing their ideas graphically can disrupt flow in a research project. Here, too, Shared Drawing can allow the collective mind to support the individual. Here are examples of some other possible uses for the protocol:

- ♦ You notice that some of the children want to draw people, but their representation isn't particularly satisfying for them. Using the protocol can allow them to benefit from the insight of more experienced children.
- ♦ A child who is trying to represent a person riding a horse finds that he needs a different way of drawing a person than the straight-on, arms-out stick figures he's been drawing. With your support, he can invite other children to a Shared Drawing session to think with him about the problem. Multiple minds on the challenge can lead to a richer learning experience for all.
- ♦ A child's representation is not evolving or becoming more sophisticated over time. Using the protocol may help her take the risks necessary for growth.
- ♦ A child is showing signs of frustration when drawing. He may be in an in-between space, where what used to satisfy him no longer does, but he doesn't yet have the skill or confidence to move forward. A Shared Drawing session allows him to be privy to the thinking of more experienced children and to be exposed to their understanding of drawing without the pressure of wielding the pen himself. It may give him the courage he needs to draw or to ask for help with drawing.

The Study Protocol

The Study Protocol is useful when a teacher notices that a child avoids drawing (or representing with any media, but we will use drawing as an example here), throws attempt after attempt away, declares intent to draw something but renames it when it turns out to look like something else, cries in frustration, or asks someone to draw for her. This can happen when a child develops the desire to represent before she knows how, and no adult recognizes her need for support. Left to face the dilemma alone, she develops coping mechanisms that can keep her from trying. The Study Protocol can be the support she needs. Like the Shared Drawing Protocol, the Study Protocol is for both teachers and children. It is support for a teacher when he wants to help a child who is struggling to represent her idea and a protocol that a child eventually can use to help herself. It gives the child an alternative to giving up on her intent to represent something and can keep the process cognitive so that she is less likely to abandon her intent due to frustration or other unpleasant emotions. Here's how the protocol goes, using drawing as an example.

- ◆ The child declares intent to draw something, or you observe the child setting out to do so. You notice, but don't intervene unless she seems to be stuck, either getting ready to give up on her intention, showing signs of frustration, or showing some other sign of being dissatisfied. It is important to distinguish the child's dissatisfaction from your own idea of what the drawing should be. The essential task of the teacher is to help the child realize her intent with the least amount of intervention possible. If the child is stuck:
- ◆ The teacher approaches and invites the child into dialogue about the drawing. She does not tell or show the child how to draw or offer to draw for him. Rather, she takes a listening stance. She asks herself, "Where's the sticking point?" There are several possibilities.
  - The child does not have a complete enough mental image of the object to draw it.
  - She knows what the object "has," but can't organize the task.
  - She doesn't have enough experience drawing the necessary shapes and isn't confident.
  - She struggles to control the pen.
  - She is lacking the confidence to try.

♦ The teacher reassures the child that he will help her until she is satisfied with her drawing (and he must follow through). Once he understands where the sticking point is, he can lend the child the resources she needs.

To learn what is creating inner conflict for the child, the teacher asks her a series of questions.

♦ "What does a _____ have?" If the child can't answer, or her answer is incomplete, then the teacher might hypothesize that the child could use a more comprehensive mental image of the object. The teacher might offer the child a referent. Here is a story by way of example.

Lily wanted to make a three-dimensional bed out of recycled materials. She gathered the materials she thought she'd need but then sat in front of them for a while, apparently stuck. Initiating the protocol, I asked Lily what a bed had. 'Blankets and a pillow,' Lily recalled. When asked, she couldn't say what else a bed had. This exchange made me wonder if Lily's mental image of a bed was complete enough for her to represent it to her satisfaction. Knowing that sometimes, when a five-year-old can't articulate her thoughts, she can represent them graphically, I invited her to draw a bed. Indeed, Lily drew a pillow and a blanket, separate from each other. No wonder she was stuck! Though she certainly had plenty of experience with her own bed, her mental image was limited.

Though Lily's intent was to construct a three-dimensional bed, she had more experience drawing than constructing with the recycled materials she'd chosen, so we stuck to drawing as a rehearsal for making the bed. Since she did not have a complete mental image of 'bed,' I wanted to offer her a referent, and I hypothesized that she needed not a drawing or photo of a bed but a three-dimensional model. Without a toy bed available, I recalled that there were actual beds on another part of campus, so she and I took a 'field trip' so Lily could study the bed through drawing. My role, as I saw it, was to find Lily the referent she needed and support her attempt to see all the parts of the bed and their relationship to each other. (It is not always the case that moving from three dimensions to two and back to three is helpful. I made this invitation based on what I knew about Lily and her ability to make those leaps). Lily studied the real-life bed through drawing and, when she returned to the classroom, was able to construct a three-dimensional bed to her satisfaction.

Lily's bed story illustrates a situation in which, when a child needs a more complete mental image of a subject, you can ask her if she would like to look at a model or picture of the object she is trying to draw. You might have a collection of photographs and line drawings to call upon as referents, or you can do a safe search for a referent on a computer or iPad with the child. You can negotiate which image will be most helpful as a referent. I usually had a sense of the kind of image that would be most helpful as a referent (e.g., a tiger in profile or straight on, or a line drawing vs. a photograph), and it was the child who was developing a mental image, so we would navigate the choice of referent together.

- ♦ If the child can tell you what the subject of his drawing "has" but still is stuck, you might wonder if she is in conflict around the organization of the task. You can ask her, "What part will you draw first?" and, perhaps, "What shape is that part?" The child wields the pen, and the decisions are hers. You are simply helping her organize the task a bit while supplementing her confidence as needed.

The study Lily drew from life and the bed she constructed once she had a more complete mental image of "bed."

- As the child draws, your physical presence is co-regulating. Just by being present, you are sending the message, "I know you can do this, and I will stay with you until you are okay doing this alone." I often found that if I left too soon, the child who was drawing and feeling successful might abandon the task. There's an art to knowing when the child can continue on her own with confidence, and you will make mistakes as you learn about that child and her optimism around drawing. Those mistakes are the way you learn when and whether a child is comfortable without your presence.
- Sometimes a child will be dissatisfied with an attempt at a part of a drawing. When that happens, you can help her sustain her effort by inviting her to label her first attempt with the number 1 (she can write it, or you can help), keep that attempt beside her, and then start again. If she is still dissatisfied with the second attempt, she will label it "2" and so on until she is satisfied with her drawing. The numbers are to honor her attempts and help her see her progress later. The child can do this with the entire drawing, or you can invite her to create a work page where she uses the Study Protocol with an element of the drawing she finds challenging. Say she is dissatisfied with the body of a horse she is drawing. You might invite her to get another piece of paper and draw the body there. She makes as many attempts as necessary, numbering each until she is satisfied. By working out how to draw the body on a separate piece of paper, she is avoiding the clutter on her original drawing, which could discourage her. Meanwhile, you can support her efforts using the Study Protocol.

Whether she makes her attempts whole (i.e., draws the horse but stops and restarts when she realizes it's not looking the way she wants it to) or makes separate studies of challenging parts, she keeps all the attempts, honoring them as her drawing teachers. We do use the term "satisfied" with the children. Sometimes, at first, children learn to say they are satisfied when they are not. But the protocol encourages deep enough engagement in efforts toward their intent that most children do come to care about being satisfied with their representations.

Isabelle wanted to draw a praying mantis from life. Her first attempt left her dissatisfied (see below). Seeing this, I approached and asked if she would like some help. She accepted the offer and all I did was help Isabelle's eye connect with the parts of the praying mantis in the box. The result was her second attempt, with which she was satisfied, or so I thought. A bit later, though, Isabelle returned to the task, fortified enough to give the drawing…and the process…another go.

- ◆ Work toward a reasonable satisfaction bar. Your encouraging presence and the tacit or spoken message to the child that you will stay and help as long as she needs you is a way of lending confidence to try. But if she is to rely on her own confidence, she will need a satisfaction bar that allows for risk taking and engagement. Even by five years old, children may have already developed coping strategies to deal with their frustration over a gap between their desire to represent an object or idea and their skillset. Often children would enter my junior kindergarten class with little experience with graphic media. They came with a small repertoire of figures they knew how to draw like houses, flowers, rainbows, or stick figures. They did not know that they could represent anything they could think. Though we opened that door for them, we saw that some children were stymied by the belief that they did not know how to draw. The underconfident might not choose to draw/paint, etc., at all. Or they might start to draw but then crumple up and throw away try after try. Some would declare intent to make something but abandon their plan easily when their frog looked like a blob; they just said, "Well, actually, it's a blob." Some cried in frustration. And some just didn't engage with the process. They might choose to draw but put one small scribble on the page and start another, on repeat. The Study Protocol offered children and teachers support so that the children could stick with their intent and work toward satisfaction.

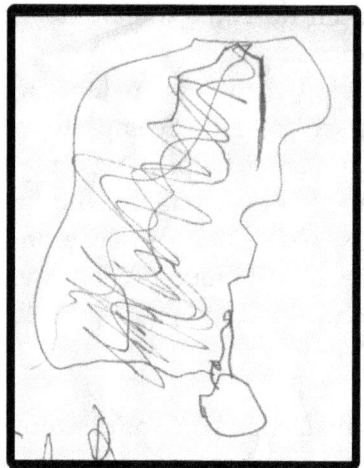
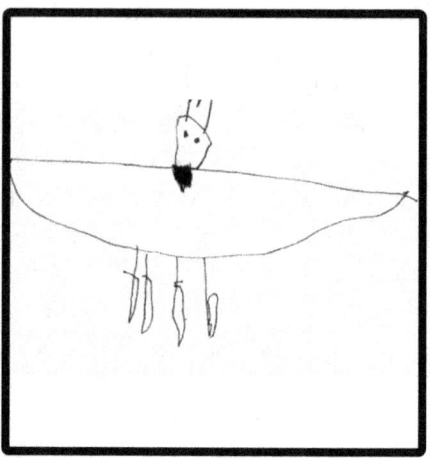

Isabelle had seemed satisfied with her second drawing of a praying mantis, above. But later she returned to the task and used the Study Protocol on her own.

Now and again, you may find that a child's satisfaction bar doesn't serve her well. If her satisfaction bar is too high, she will never be pleased with her work, and her confidence may take a hit. If her satisfaction bar is too low, it could hinder her growth. This was the case with the child who put a quick scribble on each page and declared herself satisfied. In these situations, you can teach the child the Study Protocol to help her accomplish her goals.

For the child who is never satisfied, it might be enough to teach her the study protocol. If she needs more support, you can review her previous representations with her to point out where she started and what she can do so much better now. When she expresses displeasure with her work, you can help her articulate what about her work isn't what she'd hoped, ask her what she'd like to do about that aspect of the piece, and facilitate whatever you come up with together. That might be creating a working page so the child can study that one element until she is satisfied. Or it might be inviting the child to represent the hard thing in another graphic language first. Such situations require a teacher's creativity. Whatever the solution, let it be collaborative, with the child and the teacher together.

If a child's satisfaction bar is too low to support growth, you can sit with her and listen to her plan (does she have one?). If she is still exploring the medium, it may be inappropriate to expect her to represent with it at all. But if she articulates a desire to make something with the medium, she may be able to benefit from having you beside her, asking her about her intent, offering emotional support, and, at times, challenging her. You might ask her to tell you about what she is planning to represent. If her response leaves room for your support, you can use the Study Protocol. If not, use the interchange as information about the child and her thinking.

The teacher's response to children's representations has the power to inspire and the power to shut down. Of course, we want the former. Still, many teachers gush over every picture, tell the child what's good about the painting, or guess incorrectly what the child has represented. Any of these responses, as well-meaning as they might be, positions an assessment of the child's work squarely from the teacher's perspective. And they all preclude the opportunity to hear and understand a bit more about the child's thinking. Instead, consider asking a story question. That is, a question whose answer might well be a story instead of no response or a one-word response. When children show me their work, I often ask, "What's happening here?" The question is ambiguous enough that it could mean, "Tell me about your process," "What is the story you are telling?" or any number of expressions of interest. When children answer the question, they re-engage with a piece that they thought they had finished. They may start to tell you what's happening in their work and suddenly declare, "Oh! I forgot the _____" and revisit their work. The disposition to revisit and revise because they are interested in creating a more complete representation of an idea has long-term implications for learning.

Sometimes, the challenge to represent something tricky is a group process. Up next is a story of a small group's intent to represent collaboratively and how they went about extending their study and solving their problems.

References

Forman, G. (1994). "Different Media, Different Languages" in Katz, L. & Cesaraone, B., eds. *Reflections on the Reggio Emilia Approach*, ERIC/EECE.

Gandini, L. (2005). "From the Beginning of the Atelier to Materials as Languages: Conversations from Reggio Emilia" in Gandini, L., Hill, L., Cadwell, L. & Schwall, C., eds. *In the Spirit of the Studio*. Teachers College Press.

Rinaldi, C. (2005). "The Whole School as an Atelier: Reflections by Carla Rinaldi" in Gandini, L, Hill, L, Cadwell, L. & Schwall, C, eds. *In the Spirit of the Studio*. Teachers College Press. 169.

Routman, R. (1991). *Invitations: Changing as Teachers and Learners K-12*. Heinemann. 59.

14

The Clay Horse

This is the story of a small group of five-year-old girls who declared intent to represent something and encountered a sticking point that threatened to derail the project. The children and their teacher used the representation protocols so that the small group could continue to work through the problem. The protocols not only served as guides forward, but because the children had come to understand the possibilities the protocols provided (there *is* a solution; this is just a problem to solve), they avoided the emotional dam that could have ended the project altogether.

> Sophia loved horses. She wore shirts with horses, her toys were horses, she talked about horses, and she chose horse books at the library. Sophia's classmates saw 'horse' as part of her identity (never mind that she had never been on a horse or knew any horses, as we later discovered). We had a tradition of making gifts for children's birthdays. These gifts were always conceived and created by a small group of the birthday child's friends. When it came time to choose what to make for Sophia on her birthday, her friends did not hesitate: a horse, they said, life-sized if possible. Of course, the horse did not end up life-sized… but this small group project turned out to be a life-sized investigation for the entire class.

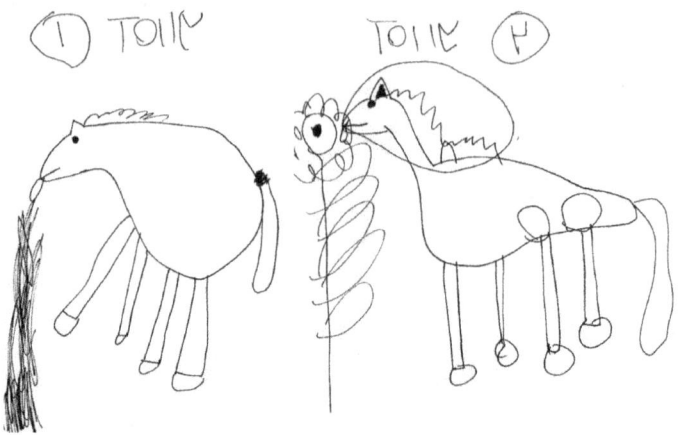

Tolly has used the Study Protocol to learn about horse anatomy. These are her first and fourth studies.

The small group that gathered to make the horse determined that clay would be the best medium for the project. Once they settled on subject and medium, we talked a bit about the necessity of developing a shared image of 'horse,' for what would happen if Tolly had one idea of 'horse' in her head but Amelia had a different one, and Callie another, and Shepard another, and they all set out to work on the same clay horse? Someone acknowledged that it would surely fall down. And so, we set out to develop each child's individual image of 'horse' and, at the same time, a shared one. At first with no referents, and later with photographs and a realistic toy horse to look at, the children drew horses, trying to refine their understanding of what a horse has and where.

When the small group felt ready, they chose one of their drawings to use as a referent and began working with the clay. They worked with enthusiasm for a few days. Then, as the horse was taking shape, one of the children declared, 'This isn't working. It looks like a giraffe!' The others agreed, and they seemed deflated. I knew the project was in danger of stalling. So, I turned to a flexible protocol and invited the children to seek support from the rest of the class. In my experience, if my timing is

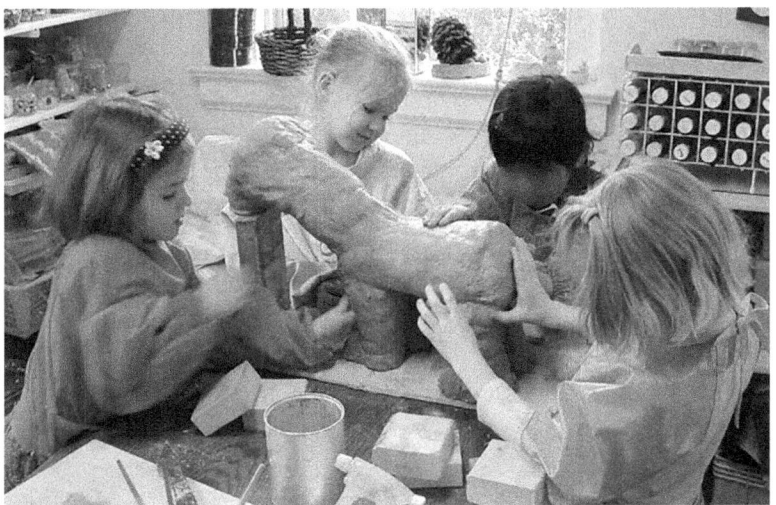

Shortly after this picture was taken, the children declared their dissatisfaction with the sculpture. "It looks like a giraffe!" they exclaimed.

good and I have not intervened too soon or waited so long that interest suffered, children are usually happy to take problems to the whole group.

We held the next class meeting in the studio. The small group explained their intent, articulated the problem, and asked their classmates for help. After some outpouring of possible solutions, the class agreed to help the small group understand 'horseness' better. 'How will you do that?' I asked. The children reasoned that if they could figure out how to represent horses, they could explain how it is done to the original small group. Over many days, all the children drew, painted, and sculpted horses using no referent and both two-dimensional and three-dimensional models.

All the children in the class were busy studying horses by drawing, painting, and sculpting from memory, books, and realistic toy horses children brought from home. But we realized that some of the these city dwellers had never seen a live horse up close. Thinking it might enrich their image of 'horse,' we arranged a visit to a horse farm, where we had some close encounters with horses, including mares with foals. We brought clipboards and 'thinking pens' (black felt-tip pens), and the children sketched from life. When we returned, the children's enthusiasm for representing horses in multiple media swelled. We teachers obliged by providing materials for new explorations of 'horseness' for as long as the children showed interest.

As a result, 'horse' became a part of the culture of the class, a part of our daily life. With long periods of self-directed activity every day, the children expressed their passion by choosing to represent their growing understandings, questions, confusions, and perspectives through the many media available to them. Had we not given time and space for such explorations and had we not provided a wide range of materials, we would not have learned as much about the children and what set their intellects on fire. At this time, they were virtually shouting 'Horse!' in their representations.

Sometimes the children disagreed about how to represent parts of a horse. At one point, they found themselves in cognitive conflict over how to draw a hoof. Recognizing an opportunity, I gathered the children in front of a chalkboard, let them know about the argument I heard, and invited dialogue about the differences of opinion. Is the

Three children with an idea to paint a horse mural negotiated a plan (their drawing is taped to the fence). Here they execute their plan on the acrylic easel in the outdoor classroom.

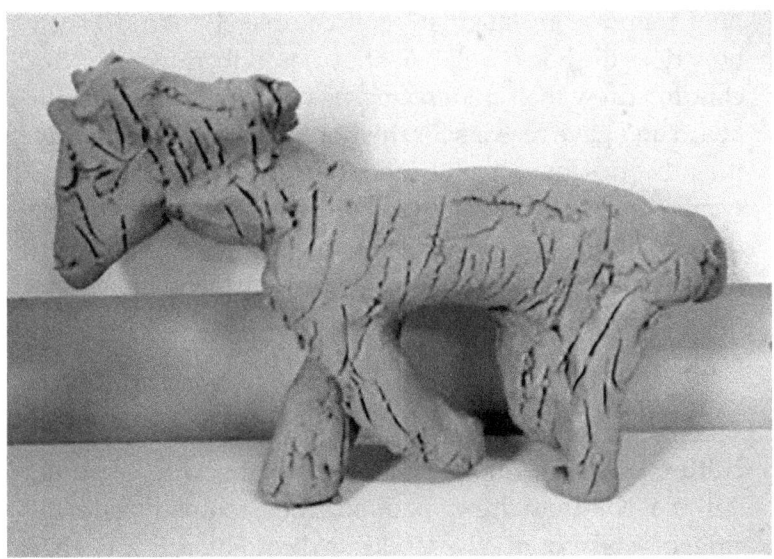

A child's study of a moving horse in clay.

A child combines two media to represent the horse she is imagining -- tempera paint and oil pastels.

hoof round or rectangular? Is it completely round? Then how does the horse walk? As they posed their theories, the children drew their understandings of 'hoof' on the chalkboard and gave reasons for their opinions, giving clarity to their theories for each other and for themselves. In this way, conflict born of a diversity of perspectives led to deeper understanding and cleared the way for more sophisticated representation. In time, as their horse drawings became more and more accurate and detailed, the children expressed increasing satisfaction with their efforts.

The life-sized-horse small group benefitted from the culture of 'horse' that developed in the whole group. All the children drew, painted, and sculpted side by side or collaboratively. Children brought artifacts that they (or their parents, who were also involved) thought would be helpful to the project. The children collaboratively constructed knowledge about how a horse's body 'works.' After many weeks of investigation and with the

Drawings made after the children had represented horses many times in multiple languages.

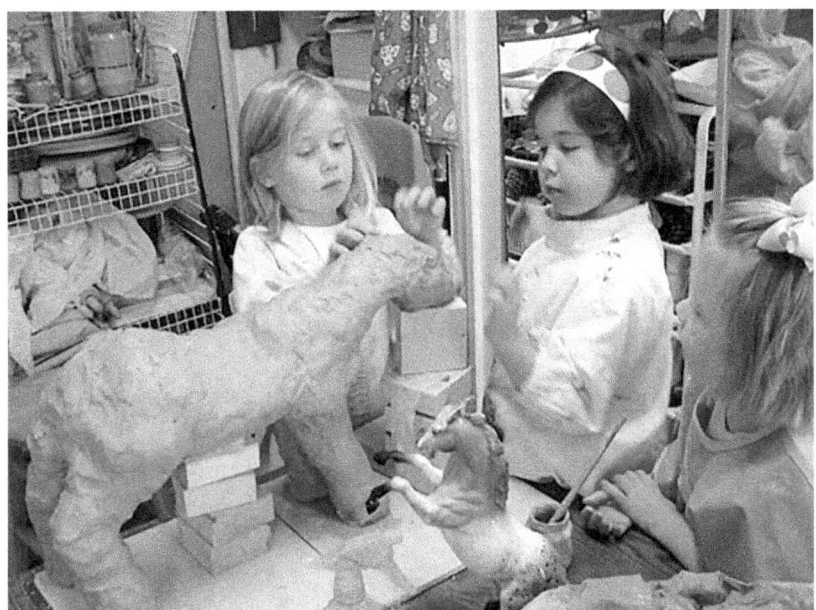

The children were satisfied with the second iteration of the clay horse.

intelligence of the whole group to support them, the small group felt ready to try again. The group membership shuffled itself a bit, with some of the original members choosing to leave but others choosing to join. They started sculpting again, armed with increased knowledge about the anatomy of a horse and buoyed by the support of the whole class.

The Clay Horse investigation lasted many weeks. Its energy flowed from small group to large group, back again, and back yet again, in a way that many such investigations do. Making the work of the small group public, through documentation and presentations by the small project group, helped get the energy unstuck, transcended sticky problems, and re-inspired and re-focused the work. When the small group went to the large group for help they pulled all the into the investigation of 'horseness,' creating a shared long-term interest that permeated play, conversation, and representation.

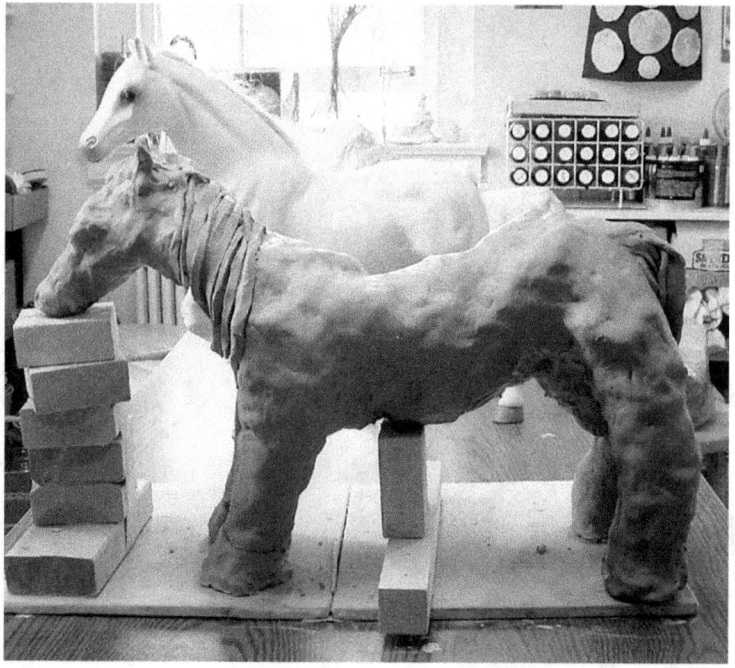

The final clay horse beside one of the models the children used as a referent.

Consider This

- While the children in your class are drawing, take note of the children who seem to struggle to represent their ideas. Notice expressions of frustration, reluctance to venture beyond a few familiar figures, avoidance of drawing, painting, or sculpting, or any other struggle. Ask yourself what protocol in this chapter might support each of those children and their growing competence and confidence in representing their ideas.
- Choose one child who is struggling with drawing something he wants to represent. Ask yourself the preliminary questions in the protocol and then introduce the study protocol to him. Do this while other children are working nearby, so that they are witness to the process.
- Collect examples of children's drawings of human figures over several days. Then hold a Shared Drawing session

with a group of children to co-construct the human figure. Afterward, pay attention to the children's spontaneous individual drawings over several more days. Do you notice any difference in the children's drawings of people? If so, the timing of the Shared Drawing session was just right for those children.

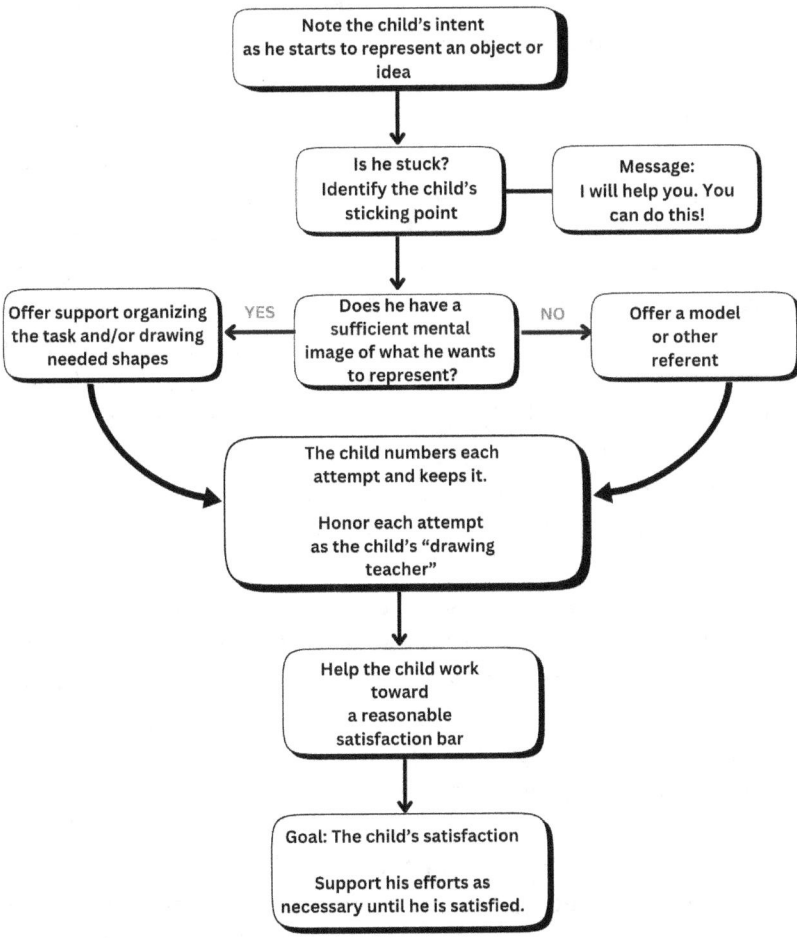

The Study Protocol.

Conclusion

The flexible protocols in this book are not to be considered a curriculum or a list or a description of an instructional method. Rather, they are tools for the back pocket of the thinking teacher. Some may be tempted to treat them as scripts, in which case they are no better than scripts. Remember the analogy of a forest hike? I hope that you will think of the protocols in this book as guiding signs along an unfamiliar woodland path. Your research with children is that meandering path. You may know where you began but have no idea where it's leading or the route it will take. You might consider the hike in the woods an adventure. You take the journey with an awake mind because it is a new experience. The fact that the path splits deep in the woods, presenting a choice toward an unknown end, is both exciting and maybe a bit scary, but the emotion you feel at the crossroads further awakens your mind. You respond with joy to little surprises along the hike, like a deer sighting or a sudden flower. And every now and again, a trail sign supports your navigation or informs you in some way, but the signs never prescribe a thing. And so it is with children's research and the guide … but not prescription … of protocols, these that are gifted to you and the ones you come up with yourself.

Flow challenges will arise wherever research with children is happening. We can expect that those challenges will feel uncomfortable. But we can also expect that we can navigate through them without derailing the research or hindering children's engagement. Knowing that can help us abide the inner conflict of not knowing where we will end up. We can expect to be amazed at the brilliance we witness as children engage deeply with ideas. We can know that there will be times when we are surprised by joy along the path. And we can trust that, in the end, what the children and teachers learn through the process will far exceed anything a disconnected curriculum publisher or school administrator could ever prescribe. Anticipating the conflict that resides in sticking points and the joy inherent in this way of working alongside children and other teachers makes it all worthwhile.

I hope this book has given you food for thought and inspiration to investigate the flow challenges you encounter. I also hope that you will construct your own flexible protocols and share them with the education community. Perhaps, in time, we can retire the scripts that litter teachers' manuals and the Internet and supplant them with strategies that teach us how to proceed in a thinking, creative way. My wish is that as you use the protocols, they will become your own and that you will adapt them, grow them, and create new flexible protocols to address your own sticking points.

Teaching and learning will never be without conflict. What matters is that we shift our stance from avoiding to embracing the learning possibilities. In writing this book, I set out to illuminate a different kind of conflict that emerges when we engage in meaningful research with young children. When we control all aspects of a child's day, when we enforce adult agendas most of the time, and when we ask children to restrain their curiosity and expend energy controlling their impulses instead of engaging in inquiry, the type of conflict we encounter likely will require a teacher to manage behavior. Instead, let's listen. We can know what sets young intellects on fire by observing their responses when we invite children into collaborative research. Young children tell us what they need and are driven to do. When we fight those impulses, we are wrestling with the children. When we go with the children into imagination and inquiry, we are wrestling with ideas together. Two very different types of conflict. Two very different types of classrooms. Which do you choose?

Resources

For Those Who Are New to the Reggio Emilia Philosophy

You may want to check out the following resources.

Edwards, C., Gandini, L. & Forman, G. eds. (2012). *The Hundred Languages of Children: The Reggio Emilia Experience in Transformation* (3rd ed.). Praeger.

Fraser, S. & Gestwicki, C. (2002). *Authentic Childhood: Exploring Reggio Emilia in the Classroom*. Delmar.

Gandini, L., Hill, L., Cadwell, L. & Schwall, C. eds. (2005). *In the Spirit of the Studio: Learning from the Atelier of Reggio Emilia*. Teachers College Press.

Giudici, C., Rindaldi, C. & Krechevsky, M. (2001). *Making Learning Visible: Children as Individual and Group Learners*. Project Zero & Reggio Children.

Krechevsky, M., Mardell, B., Rivard, M. & Wilson, D. (2013). *Visible Learners: Promoting Reggio-Inspired Approaches in All Schools*. Jossie-Bass.

The North American Reggio Emilia Alliance (NAREA) publishes a quarterly journal, *Innovations in Early Education: The International Reggio Emilia Exchange*, an excellent resource for those interested in the Reggio Emilia Approach.

Resources for Inspiration about Learning Spaces

https://pokenwright.com/blog/resources-for-learning-spaces/

Ceppi, G. and Zini, M. (1998) *Children, Spaces, Relations. Metaproject for an Environment for Young Children*. Domus Academy Research Center.

Wonderful images in videos from L'Atelier in Miami, FL on their website, particularly of the toddler and preschool classrooms: https://www.latelier.org/latelier.html.

For Product Safety Concerns and Information please contact our EU
representative GPSR@taylorandfrancis.com
Taylor & Francis Verlag GmbH, Kaufingerstraße 24, 80331 München, Germany

www.ingramcontent.com/pod-product-compliance
Lightning Source LLC
Chambersburg PA
CBHW070400240426
43661CB00056B/2482